C-2308   CAREER EXAMINATION SERIES

*This is your
PASSBOOK for...*

Highway General Foreman

*Test Preparation Study Guide
Questions & Answers*

COPYRIGHT NOTICE

This book is SOLELY intended for, is sold ONLY to, and its use is RESTRICTED to individual, bona fide applicants or candidates who qualify by virtue of having seriously filed applications for appropriate license, certificate, professional and/or promotional advancement, higher school matriculation, scholarship, or other legitimate requirements of education and/or governmental authorities.

This book is NOT intended for use, class instruction, tutoring, training, duplication, copying, reprinting, excerption, or adaptation, etc., by:

1) Other publishers
2) Proprietors and/or Instructors of "Coaching" and/or Preparatory Courses
3) Personnel and/or Training Divisions of commercial, industrial, and governmental organizations
4) Schools, colleges, or universities and/or their departments and staffs, including teachers and other personnel
5) Testing Agencies or Bureaus
6) Study groups which seek by the purchase of a single volume to copy and/or duplicate and/or adapt this material for use by the group as a whole without having purchased individual volumes for each of the members of the group
7) Et al.

Such persons would be in violation of appropriate Federal and State statutes.

PROVISION OF LICENSING AGREEMENTS – Recognized educational, commercial, industrial, and governmental institutions and organizations, and others legitimately engaged in educational pursuits, including training, testing, and measurement activities, may address request for a licensing agreement to the copyright owners, who will determine whether, and under what conditions, including fees and charges, the materials in this book may be used them. In other words, a licensing facility exists for the legitimate use of the material in this book on other than an individual basis. However, it is asseverated and affirmed here that the material in this book CANNOT be used without the receipt of the express permission of such a licensing agreement from the Publishers. Inquiries re licensing should be addressed to the company, attention rights and permissions department.

All rights reserved, including the right of reproduction in whole or in part, in any form or by any means, electronic or mechanical, including photocopying, recording, or by any information storage and retrieval system, without permission in writing from the Publisher.

Copyright © 2024 by
National Learning Corporation

212 Michael Drive, Syosset, NY 11791
(516) 921-8888 • www.passbooks.com
E-mail: info@passbooks.com

PUBLISHED IN THE UNITED STATES OF AMERICA

PASSBOOK® SERIES

THE *PASSBOOK® SERIES* has been created to prepare applicants and candidates for the ultimate academic battlefield – the examination room.

At some time in our lives, each and every one of us may be required to take an examination – for validation, matriculation, admission, qualification, registration, certification, or licensure.

Based on the assumption that every applicant or candidate has met the basic formal educational standards, has taken the required number of courses, and read the necessary texts, the *PASSBOOK® SERIES* furnishes the one special preparation which may assure passing with confidence, instead of failing with insecurity. Examination questions – together with answers – are furnished as the basic vehicle for study so that the mysteries of the examination and its compounding difficulties may be eliminated or diminished by a sure method.

This book is meant to help you pass your examination provided that you qualify and are serious in your objective.

The entire field is reviewed through the huge store of content information which is succinctly presented through a provocative and challenging approach – the question-and-answer method.

A climate of success is established by furnishing the correct answers at the end of each test.

You soon learn to recognize types of questions, forms of questions, and patterns of questioning. You may even begin to anticipate expected outcomes.

You perceive that many questions are repeated or adapted so that you can gain acute insights, which may enable you to score many sure points.

You learn how to confront new questions, or types of questions, and to attack them confidently and work out the correct answers.

You note objectives and emphases, and recognize pitfalls and dangers, so that you may make positive educational adjustments.

Moreover, you are kept fully informed in relation to new concepts, methods, practices, and directions in the field.

You discover that you are actually taking the examination all the time: you are preparing for the examination by "taking" an examination, not by reading extraneous and/or supererogatory textbooks.

In short, this PASSBOOK®, used directedly, should be an important factor in helping you to pass your test.

HIGHWAY GENERAL FOREMAN

DISTINGUISHING FEATURES OF THE CLASS:
   This position is responsible for supervising the work of a highway crew, to insure that work is accomplished in an efficient manner, on schedule and according to approved procedures. Specific instructions are received from the town or county highway department pertaining to a work schedule and upon completion, a personal inspection is made and report made on the project. The General Foreman outlines and plans the work to be performed and maintains constant check on the progress. Supervision is exercised over assistant foreman, road maintenance foreman and other highway maintenance workers.

TYPICAL WORK ACTIVITIES (illustrative only)
   These include but are not limited to the following: Plans and coordinates work activities of all highway maintenance employees; Plans and supervises the building and repair of county roads; Inspects work activities of highway crews; Oversees snow removal activities; Assigns and plans the use of automotive and road maintenance equipment; Directs the repair and maintenance of catch basins and drains; Plans and supervises the repair and maintenance of bridges and buildings; Makes decisions in the absence of the Commissioner. Full performance, knowledge, skills, abilities and personal characteristics required of candidate are as follows: Thorough knowledge of methods of road maintenance and repair; good knowledge of repair and maintenance of bridges and buildings; ability to plan and supervise the work of others; ability to keep accurate records and make necessary reports; ability to follow written and oral instructions; ability to make correct arithmetic computations; reliability; mental alertness; physical condition commensurate with the demands of the position.

SUBJECTS OF EXAMINATION:
The written test designed to evaluate knowledge, skills and /or abilities in the following areas:
   1. **Administrative supervision** -These questions test for knowledge of the principles and practices involved in directing the activities of a large subordinate staff, including subordinate supervisors. Questions relate to the personal interactions between an upper level supervisor and his/her subordinate supervisors in the accomplishment of objectives. These questions cover such areas as assigning work to and coordinating the activities of several units, establishing and guiding staff development programs, evaluating the performance of subordinate supervisors, and maintaining relationships with other organizational sections.
   2. **Bridge reconstruction, maintenance, and repair**-These questions test for knowledge of the proper methods, materials, and equipment used in the upkeep of bridges and bridge abutments, including concrete and pavement maintenance; protective sealants and waterproofing; scour protection; steel maintenance, sandblasting, painting, and welding; environmental and worker protection safeguards; inspection principles and procedures; and snow and ice removal and control.
   3. **Highways, drainage facilities, related structures, and snow and ice control** -These questions test for knowledge of practices and materials used in the maintenance and repair of highway-related structures and may include such areas as roadway surfaces, shoulders, embankments, drainage materials, guide rails, highway maintenance equipment, and ice and snow removal and control.

4. **Safety practices** - These questions test for knowledge of and the ability to apply safety principles related to construction and maintenance work zones, including traffic control, the safe use of equipment, and the overall safety of workers, the traveling public, and the work environment.
5. **Scheduling work and equipment** - These questions test for knowledge of work scheduling principles and for the ability to arrange work and equipment assignments in a manner that will achieve work goals while staying within scheduling criteria. This may include setting up vacation or work schedules taking into consideration such factors as seniority, work skills, duty hours, and shift coverage.
6. **Understanding and interpreting plans, specifications, and technical instructions** - The questions test for the ability to comprehend, analyze, and perform computations based on technical drawings and written presentations related to construction and maintenance projects. All the information needed to answer the questions will be provided in the written material and/or drawings.

HOW TO TAKE A TEST

I. YOU MUST PASS AN EXAMINATION

A. WHAT EVERY CANDIDATE SHOULD KNOW

Examination applicants often ask us for help in preparing for the written test. What can I study in advance? What kinds of questions will be asked? How will the test be given? How will the papers be graded?

As an applicant for a civil service examination, you may be wondering about some of these things. Our purpose here is to suggest effective methods of advance study and to describe civil service examinations.

Your chances for success on this examination can be increased if you know how to prepare. Those "pre-examination jitters" can be reduced if you know what to expect. You can even experience an adventure in good citizenship if you know why civil service exams are given.

B. WHY ARE CIVIL SERVICE EXAMINATIONS GIVEN?

Civil service examinations are important to you in two ways. As a citizen, you want public jobs filled by employees who know how to do their work. As a job seeker, you want a fair chance to compete for that job on an equal footing with other candidates. The best-known means of accomplishing this two-fold goal is the competitive examination.

Exams are widely publicized throughout the nation. They may be administered for jobs in federal, state, city, municipal, town or village governments or agencies.

Any citizen may apply, with some limitations, such as the age or residence of applicants. Your experience and education may be reviewed to see whether you meet the requirements for the particular examination. When these requirements exist, they are reasonable and applied consistently to all applicants. Thus, a competitive examination may cause you some uneasiness now, but it is your privilege and safeguard.

C. HOW ARE CIVIL SERVICE EXAMS DEVELOPED?

Examinations are carefully written by trained technicians who are specialists in the field known as "psychological measurement," in consultation with recognized authorities in the field of work that the test will cover. These experts recommend the subject matter areas or skills to be tested; only those knowledges or skills important to your success on the job are included. The most reliable books and source materials available are used as references. Together, the experts and technicians judge the difficulty level of the questions.

Test technicians know how to phrase questions so that the problem is clearly stated. Their ethics do not permit "trick" or "catch" questions. Questions may have been tried out on sample groups, or subjected to statistical analysis, to determine their usefulness.

Written tests are often used in combination with performance tests, ratings of training and experience, and oral interviews. All of these measures combine to form the best-known means of finding the right person for the right job.

II. HOW TO PASS THE WRITTEN TEST

A. NATURE OF THE EXAMINATION

To prepare intelligently for civil service examinations, you should know how they differ from school examinations you have taken. In school you were assigned certain definite pages to read or subjects to cover. The examination questions were quite detailed and usually emphasized memory. Civil service exams, on the other hand, try to discover your present ability to perform the duties of a position, plus your potentiality to learn these duties. In other words, a civil service exam attempts to predict how successful you will be. Questions cover such a broad area that they cannot be as minute and detailed as school exam questions.

In the public service similar kinds of work, or positions, are grouped together in one "class." This process is known as *position-classification*. All the positions in a class are paid according to the salary range for that class. One class title covers all of these positions, and they are all tested by the same examination.

B. FOUR BASIC STEPS

1) Study the announcement

How, then, can you know what subjects to study? Our best answer is: "Learn as much as possible about the class of positions for which you've applied." The exam will test the knowledge, skills and abilities needed to do the work.

Your most valuable source of information about the position you want is the official exam announcement. This announcement lists the training and experience qualifications. Check these standards and apply only if you come reasonably close to meeting them.

The brief description of the position in the examination announcement offers some clues to the subjects which will be tested. Think about the job itself. Review the duties in your mind. Can you perform them, or are there some in which you are rusty? Fill in the blank spots in your preparation.

Many jurisdictions preview the written test in the exam announcement by including a section called "Knowledge and Abilities Required," "Scope of the Examination," or some similar heading. Here you will find out specifically what fields will be tested.

2) Review your own background

Once you learn in general what the position is all about, and what you need to know to do the work, ask yourself which subjects you already know fairly well and which need improvement. You may wonder whether to concentrate on improving your strong areas or on building some background in your fields of weakness. When the announcement has specified "some knowledge" or "considerable knowledge," or has used adjectives like "beginning principles of..." or "advanced ... methods," you can get a clue as to the number and difficulty of questions to be asked in any given field. More questions, and hence broader coverage, would be included for those subjects which are more important in the work. Now weigh your strengths and weaknesses against the job requirements and prepare accordingly.

3) Determine the level of the position

Another way to tell how intensively you should prepare is to understand the level of the job for which you are applying. Is it the entering level? In other words, is this the position in which beginners in a field of work are hired? Or is it an intermediate or advanced level? Sometimes this is indicated by such words as "Junior" or "Senior" in the class title. Other jurisdictions use Roman numerals to designate the level – Clerk I, Clerk II, for example. The word "Supervisor" sometimes appears in the title. If the level is not indicated by the title, check the description of duties. Will you be working under very close supervision, or will you have responsibility for independent decisions in this work?

4) Choose appropriate study materials

Now that you know the subjects to be examined and the relative amount of each subject to be covered, you can choose suitable study materials. For beginning level jobs, or even advanced ones, if you have a pronounced weakness in some aspect of your training, read a modern, standard textbook in that field. Be sure it is up to date and has general coverage. Such books are normally available at your library, and the librarian will be glad to help you locate one. For entry-level positions, questions of appropriate difficulty are chosen – neither highly advanced questions, nor those too simple. Such questions require careful thought but not advanced training.

If the position for which you are applying is technical or advanced, you will read more advanced, specialized material. If you are already familiar with the basic principles of your field, elementary textbooks would waste your time. Concentrate on advanced textbooks and technical periodicals. Think through the concepts and review difficult problems in your field.

These are all general sources. You can get more ideas on your own initiative, following these leads. For example, training manuals and publications of the government agency which employs workers in your field can be useful, particularly for technical and professional positions. A letter or visit to the government department involved may result in more specific study suggestions, and certainly will provide you with a more definite idea of the exact nature of the position you are seeking.

III. KINDS OF TESTS

Tests are used for purposes other than measuring knowledge and ability to perform specified duties. For some positions, it is equally important to test ability to make adjustments to new situations or to profit from training. In others, basic mental abilities not dependent on information are essential. Questions which test these things may not appear as pertinent to the duties of the position as those which test for knowledge and information. Yet they are often highly important parts of a fair examination. For very general questions, it is almost impossible to help you direct your study efforts. What we can do is to point out some of the more common of these general abilities needed in public service positions and describe some typical questions.

1) General information

Broad, general information has been found useful for predicting job success in some kinds of work. This is tested in a variety of ways, from vocabulary lists to questions about current events. Basic background in some field of work, such as sociology or economics, may be sampled in a group of questions. Often these are principles which have become familiar to most persons through exposure rather than through formal training. It is difficult to advise you how to study for these questions; being alert to the world around you is our best suggestion.

2) Verbal ability

An example of an ability needed in many positions is verbal or language ability. Verbal ability is, in brief, the ability to use and understand words. Vocabulary and grammar tests are typical measures of this ability. Reading comprehension or paragraph interpretation questions are common in many kinds of civil service tests. You are given a paragraph of written material and asked to find its central meaning.

3) Numerical ability
Number skills can be tested by the familiar arithmetic problem, by checking paired lists of numbers to see which are alike and which are different, or by interpreting charts and graphs. In the latter test, a graph may be printed in the test booklet which you are asked to use as the basis for answering questions.

4) Observation
A popular test for law-enforcement positions is the observation test. A picture is shown to you for several minutes, then taken away. Questions about the picture test your ability to observe both details and larger elements.

5) Following directions
In many positions in the public service, the employee must be able to carry out written instructions dependably and accurately. You may be given a chart with several columns, each column listing a variety of information. The questions require you to carry out directions involving the information given in the chart.

6) Skills and aptitudes
Performance tests effectively measure some manual skills and aptitudes. When the skill is one in which you are trained, such as typing or shorthand, you can practice. These tests are often very much like those given in business school or high school courses. For many of the other skills and aptitudes, however, no short-time preparation can be made. Skills and abilities natural to you or that you have developed throughout your lifetime are being tested.

Many of the general questions just described provide all the data needed to answer the questions and ask you to use your reasoning ability to find the answers. Your best preparation for these tests, as well as for tests of facts and ideas, is to be at your physical and mental best. You, no doubt, have your own methods of getting into an exam-taking mood and keeping "in shape." The next section lists some ideas on this subject.

IV. KINDS OF QUESTIONS

Only rarely is the "essay" question, which you answer in narrative form, used in civil service tests. Civil service tests are usually of the short-answer type. Full instructions for answering these questions will be given to you at the examination. But in case this is your first experience with short-answer questions and separate answer sheets, here is what you need to know:

1) Multiple-choice Questions
Most popular of the short-answer questions is the "multiple choice" or "best answer" question. It can be used, for example, to test for factual knowledge, ability to solve problems or judgment in meeting situations found at work.
A multiple-choice question is normally one of three types—
- It can begin with an incomplete statement followed by several possible endings. You are to find the one ending which *best* completes the statement, although some of the others may not be entirely wrong.
- It can also be a complete statement in the form of a question which is answered by choosing one of the statements listed.

- It can be in the form of a problem – again you select the best answer.

Here is an example of a multiple-choice question with a discussion which should give you some clues as to the method for choosing the right answer:

When an employee has a complaint about his assignment, the action which will *best* help him overcome his difficulty is to
  A. discuss his difficulty with his coworkers
  B. take the problem to the head of the organization
  C. take the problem to the person who gave him the assignment
  D. say nothing to anyone about his complaint

In answering this question, you should study each of the choices to find which is best. Consider choice "A" – Certainly an employee may discuss his complaint with fellow employees, but no change or improvement can result, and the complaint remains unresolved. Choice "B" is a poor choice since the head of the organization probably does not know what assignment you have been given, and taking your problem to him is known as "going over the head" of the supervisor. The supervisor, or person who made the assignment, is the person who can clarify it or correct any injustice. Choice "C" is, therefore, correct. To say nothing, as in choice "D," is unwise. Supervisors have and interest in knowing the problems employees are facing, and the employee is seeking a solution to his problem.

2) True/False Questions

The "true/false" or "right/wrong" form of question is sometimes used. Here a complete statement is given. Your job is to decide whether the statement is right or wrong.

SAMPLE: A roaming cell-phone call to a nearby city costs less than a non-roaming call to a distant city.

This statement is wrong, or false, since roaming calls are more expensive.

This is not a complete list of all possible question forms, although most of the others are variations of these common types. You will always get complete directions for answering questions. Be sure you understand *how* to mark your answers – ask questions until you do.

V. RECORDING YOUR ANSWERS

Computer terminals are used more and more today for many different kinds of exams.

For an examination with very few applicants, you may be told to record your answers in the test booklet itself. Separate answer sheets are much more common. If this separate answer sheet is to be scored by machine – and this is often the case – it is highly important that you mark your answers correctly in order to get credit.

An electronic scoring machine is often used in civil service offices because of the speed with which papers can be scored. Machine-scored answer sheets must be marked with a pencil, which will be given to you. This pencil has a high graphite content which responds to the electronic scoring machine. As a matter of fact, stray dots may register as answers, so do not let your pencil rest on the answer sheet while you are pondering the correct answer. Also, if your pencil lead breaks or is otherwise defective, ask for another.

Since the answer sheet will be dropped in a slot in the scoring machine, be careful not to bend the corners or get the paper crumpled.

The answer sheet normally has five vertical columns of numbers, with 30 numbers to a column. These numbers correspond to the question numbers in your test booklet. After each number, going across the page are four or five pairs of dotted lines. These short dotted lines have small letters or numbers above them. The first two pairs may also have a "T" or "F" above the letters. This indicates that the first two pairs only are to be used if the questions are of the true-false type. If the questions are multiple choice, disregard the "T" and "F" and pay attention only to the small letters or numbers.

Answer your questions in the manner of the sample that follows:

32. The largest city in the United States is
    A. Washington, D.C.
    B. New York City
    C. Chicago
    D. Detroit
    E. San Francisco

1) Choose the answer you think is best. (New York City is the largest, so "B" is correct.)
2) Find the row of dotted lines numbered the same as the question you are answering. (Find row number 32)
3) Find the pair of dotted lines corresponding to the answer. (Find the pair of lines under the mark "B.")
4) Make a solid black mark between the dotted lines.

VI. BEFORE THE TEST

Common sense will help you find procedures to follow to get ready for an examination. Too many of us, however, overlook these sensible measures. Indeed, nervousness and fatigue have been found to be the most serious reasons why applicants fail to do their best on civil service tests. Here is a list of reminders:

- Begin your preparation early – Don't wait until the last minute to go scurrying around for books and materials or to find out what the position is all about.
- Prepare continuously – An hour a night for a week is better than an all-night cram session. This has been definitely established. What is more, a night a week for a month will return better dividends than crowding your study into a shorter period of time.
- Locate the place of the exam – You have been sent a notice telling you when and where to report for the examination. If the location is in a different town or otherwise unfamiliar to you, it would be well to inquire the best route and learn something about the building.
- Relax the night before the test – Allow your mind to rest. Do not study at all that night. Plan some mild recreation or diversion; then go to bed early and get a good night's sleep.
- Get up early enough to make a leisurely trip to the place for the test – This way unforeseen events, traffic snarls, unfamiliar buildings, etc. will not upset you.
- Dress comfortably – A written test is not a fashion show. You will be known by number and not by name, so wear something comfortable.

- Leave excess paraphernalia at home – Shopping bags and odd bundles will get in your way. You need bring only the items mentioned in the official notice you received; usually everything you need is provided. Do not bring reference books to the exam. They will only confuse those last minutes and be taken away from you when in the test room.
- Arrive somewhat ahead of time – If because of transportation schedules you must get there very early, bring a newspaper or magazine to take your mind off yourself while waiting.
- Locate the examination room – When you have found the proper room, you will be directed to the seat or part of the room where you will sit. Sometimes you are given a sheet of instructions to read while you are waiting. Do not fill out any forms until you are told to do so; just read them and be prepared.
- Relax and prepare to listen to the instructions
- If you have any physical problem that may keep you from doing your best, be sure to tell the test administrator. If you are sick or in poor health, you really cannot do your best on the exam. You can come back and take the test some other time.

VII. AT THE TEST

The day of the test is here and you have the test booklet in your hand. The temptation to get going is very strong. Caution! There is more to success than knowing the right answers. You must know how to identify your papers and understand variations in the type of short-answer question used in this particular examination. Follow these suggestions for maximum results from your efforts:

1) Cooperate with the monitor

The test administrator has a duty to create a situation in which you can be as much at ease as possible. He will give instructions, tell you when to begin, check to see that you are marking your answer sheet correctly, and so on. He is not there to guard you, although he will see that your competitors do not take unfair advantage. He wants to help you do your best.

2) Listen to all instructions

Don't jump the gun! Wait until you understand all directions. In most civil service tests you get more time than you need to answer the questions. So don't be in a hurry. Read each word of instructions until you clearly understand the meaning. Study the examples, listen to all announcements and follow directions. Ask questions if you do not understand what to do.

3) Identify your papers

Civil service exams are usually identified by number only. You will be assigned a number; you must not put your name on your test papers. Be sure to copy your number correctly. Since more than one exam may be given, copy your exact examination title.

4) Plan your time

Unless you are told that a test is a "speed" or "rate of work" test, speed itself is usually not important. Time enough to answer all the questions will be provided, but this does not mean that you have all day. An overall time limit has been set. Divide the total time (in minutes) by the number of questions to determine the approximate time you have for each question.

5) Do not linger over difficult questions

If you come across a difficult question, mark it with a paper clip (useful to have along) and come back to it when you have been through the booklet. One caution if you do this – be sure to skip a number on your answer sheet as well. Check often to be sure that you have not lost your place and that you are marking in the row numbered the same as the question you are answering.

6) Read the questions

Be sure you know what the question asks! Many capable people are unsuccessful because they failed to *read* the questions correctly.

7) Answer all questions

Unless you have been instructed that a penalty will be deducted for incorrect answers, it is better to guess than to omit a question.

8) Speed tests

It is often better NOT to guess on speed tests. It has been found that on timed tests people are tempted to spend the last few seconds before time is called in marking answers at random – without even reading them – in the hope of picking up a few extra points. To discourage this practice, the instructions may warn you that your score will be "corrected" for guessing. That is, a penalty will be applied. The incorrect answers will be deducted from the correct ones, or some other penalty formula will be used.

9) Review your answers

If you finish before time is called, go back to the questions you guessed or omitted to give them further thought. Review other answers if you have time.

10) Return your test materials

If you are ready to leave before others have finished or time is called, take ALL your materials to the monitor and leave quietly. Never take any test material with you. The monitor can discover whose papers are not complete, and taking a test booklet may be grounds for disqualification.

VIII. EXAMINATION TECHNIQUES

1) Read the general instructions carefully. These are usually printed on the first page of the exam booklet. As a rule, these instructions refer to the timing of the examination; the fact that you should not start work until the signal and must stop work at a signal, etc. If there are any *special* instructions, such as a choice of questions to be answered, make sure that you note this instruction carefully.

2) When you are ready to start work on the examination, that is as soon as the signal has been given, read the instructions to each question booklet, underline any key words or phrases, such as *least, best, outline, describe* and the like. In this way you will tend to answer as requested rather than discover on reviewing your paper that you *listed without describing*, that you selected the *worst* choice rather than the *best* choice, etc.

3) If the examination is of the objective or multiple-choice type – that is, each question will also give a series of possible answers: A, B, C or D, and you are called upon to select the best answer and write the letter next to that answer on your answer paper – it is advisable to start answering each question in turn. There may be anywhere from 50 to 100 such questions in the three or four hours allotted and you can see how much time would be taken if you read through all the questions before beginning to answer any. Furthermore, if you come across a question or group of questions which you know would be difficult to answer, it would undoubtedly affect your handling of all the other questions.

4) If the examination is of the essay type and contains but a few questions, it is a moot point as to whether you should read all the questions before starting to answer any one. Of course, if you are given a choice – say five out of seven and the like – then it is essential to read all the questions so you can eliminate the two that are most difficult. If, however, you are asked to answer all the questions, there may be danger in trying to answer the easiest one first because you may find that you will spend too much time on it. The best technique is to answer the first question, then proceed to the second, etc.

5) Time your answers. Before the exam begins, write down the time it started, then add the time allowed for the examination and write down the time it must be completed, then divide the time available somewhat as follows:
    - If 3-1/2 hours are allowed, that would be 210 minutes. If you have 80 objective-type questions, that would be an average of 2-1/2 minutes per question. Allow yourself no more than 2 minutes per question, or a total of 160 minutes, which will permit about 50 minutes to review.
    - If for the time allotment of 210 minutes there are 7 essay questions to answer, that would average about 30 minutes a question. Give yourself only 25 minutes per question so that you have about 35 minutes to review.

6) The most important instruction is to *read each question* and make sure you know what is wanted. The second most important instruction is to *time yourself properly* so that you answer every question. The third most important instruction is to *answer every question*. Guess if you have to but include something for each question. Remember that you will receive no credit for a blank and will probably receive some credit if you write something in answer to an essay question. If you guess a letter – say "B" for a multiple-choice question – you may have guessed right. If you leave a blank as an answer to a multiple-choice question, the examiners may respect your feelings but it will not add a point to your score. Some exams may penalize you for wrong answers, so in such cases *only*, you may not want to guess unless you have some basis for your answer.

7) Suggestions
    a. Objective-type questions
        1. Examine the question booklet for proper sequence of pages and questions
        2. Read all instructions carefully
        3. Skip any question which seems too difficult; return to it after all other questions have been answered
        4. Apportion your time properly; do not spend too much time on any single question or group of questions

5. Note and underline key words – *all, most, fewest, least, best, worst, same, opposite,* etc.
6. Pay particular attention to negatives
7. Note unusual option, e.g., unduly long, short, complex, different or similar in content to the body of the question
8. Observe the use of "hedging" words – *probably, may, most likely,* etc.
9. Make sure that your answer is put next to the same number as the question
10. Do not second-guess unless you have good reason to believe the second answer is definitely more correct
11. Cross out original answer if you decide another answer is more accurate; do not erase until you are ready to hand your paper in
12. Answer all questions; guess unless instructed otherwise
13. Leave time for review

   b. Essay questions
   1. Read each question carefully
   2. Determine exactly what is wanted. Underline key words or phrases.
   3. Decide on outline or paragraph answer
   4. Include many different points and elements unless asked to develop any one or two points or elements
   5. Show impartiality by giving pros and cons unless directed to select one side only
   6. Make and write down any assumptions you find necessary to answer the questions
   7. Watch your English, grammar, punctuation and choice of words
   8. Time your answers; don't crowd material

8) Answering the essay question

Most essay questions can be answered by framing the specific response around several key words or ideas. Here are a few such key words or ideas:

M's: manpower, materials, methods, money, management
P's: purpose, program, policy, plan, procedure, practice, problems, pitfalls, personnel, public relations

   a. Six basic steps in handling problems:
   1. Preliminary plan and background development
   2. Collect information, data and facts
   3. Analyze and interpret information, data and facts
   4. Analyze and develop solutions as well as make recommendations
   5. Prepare report and sell recommendations
   6. Install recommendations and follow up effectiveness

   b. Pitfalls to avoid
   1. *Taking things for granted* – A statement of the situation does not necessarily imply that each of the elements is necessarily true; for example, a complaint may be invalid and biased so that all that can be taken for granted is that a complaint has been registered

2. *Considering only one side of a situation* – Wherever possible, indicate several alternatives and then point out the reasons you selected the best one
3. *Failing to indicate follow up* – Whenever your answer indicates action on your part, make certain that you will take proper follow-up action to see how successful your recommendations, procedures or actions turn out to be
4. *Taking too long in answering any single question* – Remember to time your answers properly

IX. AFTER THE TEST

Scoring procedures differ in detail among civil service jurisdictions although the general principles are the same. Whether the papers are hand-scored or graded by machine we have described, they are nearly always graded by number. That is, the person who marks the paper knows only the number – never the name – of the applicant. Not until all the papers have been graded will they be matched with names. If other tests, such as training and experience or oral interview ratings have been given, scores will be combined. Different parts of the examination usually have different weights. For example, the written test might count 60 percent of the final grade, and a rating of training and experience 40 percent. In many jurisdictions, veterans will have a certain number of points added to their grades.

After the final grade has been determined, the names are placed in grade order and an eligible list is established. There are various methods for resolving ties between those who get the same final grade – probably the most common is to place first the name of the person whose application was received first. Job offers are made from the eligible list in the order the names appear on it. You will be notified of your grade and your rank as soon as all these computations have been made. This will be done as rapidly as possible.

People who are found to meet the requirements in the announcement are called "eligibles." Their names are put on a list of eligible candidates. An eligible's chances of getting a job depend on how high he stands on this list and how fast agencies are filling jobs from the list.

When a job is to be filled from a list of eligibles, the agency asks for the names of people on the list of eligibles for that job. When the civil service commission receives this request, it sends to the agency the names of the three people highest on this list. Or, if the job to be filled has specialized requirements, the office sends the agency the names of the top three persons who meet these requirements from the general list.

The appointing officer makes a choice from among the three people whose names were sent to him. If the selected person accepts the appointment, the names of the others are put back on the list to be considered for future openings.

That is the rule in hiring from all kinds of eligible lists, whether they are for typist, carpenter, chemist, or something else. For every vacancy, the appointing officer has his choice of any one of the top three eligibles on the list. This explains why the person whose name is on top of the list sometimes does not get an appointment when some of the persons lower on the list do. If the appointing officer chooses the second or third eligible, the No. 1 eligible does not get a job at once, but stays on the list until he is appointed or the list is terminated.

X. HOW TO PASS THE INTERVIEW TEST

The examination for which you applied requires an oral interview test. You have already taken the written test and you are now being called for the interview test – the final part of the formal examination.

You may think that it is not possible to prepare for an interview test and that there are no procedures to follow during an interview. Our purpose is to point out some things you can do in advance that will help you and some good rules to follow and pitfalls to avoid while you are being interviewed.

What is an interview supposed to test?

The written examination is designed to test the technical knowledge and competence of the candidate; the oral is designed to evaluate intangible qualities, not readily measured otherwise, and to establish a list showing the relative fitness of each candidate – as measured against his competitors – for the position sought. Scoring is not on the basis of "right" and "wrong," but on a sliding scale of values ranging from "not passable" to "outstanding." As a matter of fact, it is possible to achieve a relatively low score without a single "incorrect" answer because of evident weakness in the qualities being measured.

Occasionally, an examination may consist entirely of an oral test – either an individual or a group oral. In such cases, information is sought concerning the technical knowledges and abilities of the candidate, since there has been no written examination for this purpose. More commonly, however, an oral test is used to supplement a written examination.

Who conducts interviews?

The composition of oral boards varies among different jurisdictions. In nearly all, a representative of the personnel department serves as chairman. One of the members of the board may be a representative of the department in which the candidate would work. In some cases, "outside experts" are used, and, frequently, a businessman or some other representative of the general public is asked to serve. Labor and management or other special groups may be represented. The aim is to secure the services of experts in the appropriate field.

However the board is composed, it is a good idea (and not at all improper or unethical) to ascertain in advance of the interview who the members are and what groups they represent. When you are introduced to them, you will have some idea of their backgrounds and interests, and at least you will not stutter and stammer over their names.

What should be done before the interview?

While knowledge about the board members is useful and takes some of the surprise element out of the interview, there is other preparation which is more substantive. It *is* possible to prepare for an oral interview – in several ways:

1) Keep a copy of your application and review it carefully before the interview

This may be the only document before the oral board, and the starting point of the interview. Know what education and experience you have listed there, and the sequence and dates of all of it. Sometimes the board will ask you to review the highlights of your experience for them; you should not have to hem and haw doing it.

2) Study the class specification and the examination announcement

Usually, the oral board has one or both of these to guide them. The qualities, characteristics or knowledges required by the position sought are stated in these documents. They offer valuable clues as to the nature of the oral interview. For example, if the job involves supervisory responsibilities, the announcement will usually indicate that knowledge of modern supervisory methods and the qualifications of the candidate as a supervisor will be tested. If so, you can expect such questions, frequently in the form of a hypothetical situation which you are expected to solve. NEVER go into an oral without knowledge of the duties and responsibilities of the job you seek.

3) Think through each qualification required

Try to visualize the kind of questions you would ask if you were a board member. How well could you answer them? Try especially to appraise your own knowledge and background in each area, *measured against the job sought*, and identify any areas in which you are weak. Be critical and realistic – do not flatter yourself.

4) Do some general reading in areas in which you feel you may be weak

For example, if the job involves supervision and your past experience has NOT, some general reading in supervisory methods and practices, particularly in the field of human relations, might be useful. Do NOT study agency procedures or detailed manuals. The oral board will be testing your understanding and capacity, not your memory.

5) Get a good night's sleep and watch your general health and mental attitude

You will want a clear head at the interview. Take care of a cold or any other minor ailment, and of course, no hangovers.

What should be done on the day of the interview?

Now comes the day of the interview itself. Give yourself plenty of time to get there. Plan to arrive somewhat ahead of the scheduled time, particularly if your appointment is in the fore part of the day. If a previous candidate fails to appear, the board might be ready for you a bit early. By early afternoon an oral board is almost invariably behind schedule if there are many candidates, and you may have to wait. Take along a book or magazine to read, or your application to review, but leave any extraneous material in the waiting room when you go in for your interview. In any event, relax and compose yourself.

The matter of dress is important. The board is forming impressions about you – from your experience, your manners, your attitude, and your appearance. Give your personal appearance careful attention. Dress your best, but not your flashiest. Choose conservative, appropriate clothing, and be sure it is immaculate. This is a business interview, and your appearance should indicate that you regard it as such. Besides, being well groomed and properly dressed will help boost your confidence.

Sooner or later, someone will call your name and escort you into the interview room. *This is it*. From here on you are on your own. It is too late for any more preparation. But remember, you asked for this opportunity to prove your fitness, and you are here because your request was granted.

What happens when you go in?

The usual sequence of events will be as follows: The clerk (who is often the board stenographer) will introduce you to the chairman of the oral board, who will introduce you to the other members of the board. Acknowledge the introductions before you sit down. Do not be surprised if you find a microphone facing you or a stenotypist sitting by. Oral interviews are usually recorded in the event of an appeal or other review.

Usually the chairman of the board will open the interview by reviewing the highlights of your education and work experience from your application – primarily for the benefit of the other members of the board, as well as to get the material into the record. Do not interrupt or comment unless there is an error or significant misinterpretation; if that is the case, do not hesitate. But do not quibble about insignificant matters. Also, he will usually ask you some question about your education, experience or your present job – partly to get you to start talking and to establish the interviewing "rapport." He may start the actual questioning, or turn it over to one of the other members. Frequently, each member undertakes the questioning on a particular area, one in which he is perhaps most competent, so you can expect each member to participate in the examination. Because time is limited, you may also expect some rather abrupt switches in the direction the questioning takes, so do not be upset by it. Normally, a board member will not pursue a single line of questioning unless he discovers a particular strength or weakness.

After each member has participated, the chairman will usually ask whether any member has any further questions, then will ask you if you have anything you wish to add. Unless you are expecting this question, it may floor you. Worse, it may start you off on an extended, extemporaneous speech. The board is not usually seeking more information. The question is principally to offer you a last opportunity to present further qualifications or to indicate that you have nothing to add. So, if you feel that a significant qualification or characteristic has been overlooked, it is proper to point it out in a sentence or so. Do not compliment the board on the thoroughness of their examination – they have been sketchy, and you know it. If you wish, merely say, "No thank you, I have nothing further to add." This is a point where you can "talk yourself out" of a good impression or fail to present an important bit of information. Remember, *you close the interview yourself.*

The chairman will then say, "That is all, Mr. _____, thank you." Do not be startled; the interview is over, and quicker than you think. Thank him, gather your belongings and take your leave. Save your sigh of relief for the other side of the door.

How to put your best foot forward
Throughout this entire process, you may feel that the board individually and collectively is trying to pierce your defenses, seek out your hidden weaknesses and embarrass and confuse you. Actually, this is not true. They are obliged to make an appraisal of your qualifications for the job you are seeking, and they want to see you in your best light. Remember, they must interview all candidates and a non-cooperative candidate may become a failure in spite of their best efforts to bring out his qualifications. Here are 15 suggestions that will help you:

1) **Be natural – Keep your attitude confident, not cocky**
If you are not confident that you can do the job, do not expect the board to be. Do not apologize for your weaknesses, try to bring out your strong points. The board is interested in a positive, not negative, presentation. Cockiness will antagonize any board member and make him wonder if you are covering up a weakness by a false show of strength.

2) **Get comfortable, but don't lounge or sprawl**
Sit erectly but not stiffly. A careless posture may lead the board to conclude that you are careless in other things, or at least that you are not impressed by the importance of the occasion. Either conclusion is natural, even if incorrect. Do not fuss with your clothing, a pencil or an ashtray. Your hands may occasionally be useful to emphasize a point; do not let them become a point of distraction.

3) **Do not wisecrack or make small talk**
This is a serious situation, and your attitude should show that you consider it as such. Further, the time of the board is limited – they do not want to waste it, and neither should you.

4) Do not exaggerate your experience or abilities

In the first place, from information in the application or other interviews and sources, the board may know more about you than you think. Secondly, you probably will not get away with it. An experienced board is rather adept at spotting such a situation, so do not take the chance.

5) If you know a board member, do not make a point of it, yet do not hide it

Certainly you are not fooling him, and probably not the other members of the board. Do not try to take advantage of your acquaintanceship – it will probably do you little good.

6) Do not dominate the interview

Let the board do that. They will give you the clues – do not assume that you have to do all the talking. Realize that the board has a number of questions to ask you, and do not try to take up all the interview time by showing off your extensive knowledge of the answer to the first one.

7) Be attentive

You only have 20 minutes or so, and you should keep your attention at its sharpest throughout. When a member is addressing a problem or question to you, give him your undivided attention. Address your reply principally to him, but do not exclude the other board members.

8) Do not interrupt

A board member may be stating a problem for you to analyze. He will ask you a question when the time comes. Let him state the problem, and wait for the question.

9) Make sure you understand the question

Do not try to answer until you are sure what the question is. If it is not clear, restate it in your own words or ask the board member to clarify it for you. However, do not haggle about minor elements.

10) Reply promptly but not hastily

A common entry on oral board rating sheets is "candidate responded readily," or "candidate hesitated in replies." Respond as promptly and quickly as you can, but do not jump to a hasty, ill-considered answer.

11) Do not be peremptory in your answers

A brief answer is proper – but do not fire your answer back. That is a losing game from your point of view. The board member can probably ask questions much faster than you can answer them.

12) Do not try to create the answer you think the board member wants

He is interested in what kind of mind you have and how it works – not in playing games. Furthermore, he can usually spot this practice and will actually grade you down on it.

13) Do not switch sides in your reply merely to agree with a board member

Frequently, a member will take a contrary position merely to draw you out and to see if you are willing and able to defend your point of view. Do not start a debate, yet do not surrender a good position. If a position is worth taking, it is worth defending.

14) Do not be afraid to admit an error in judgment if you are shown to be wrong

The board knows that you are forced to reply without any opportunity for careful consideration. Your answer may be demonstrably wrong. If so, admit it and get on with the interview.

15) Do not dwell at length on your present job

The opening question may relate to your present assignment. Answer the question but do not go into an extended discussion. You are being examined for a *new* job, not your present one. As a matter of fact, try to phrase ALL your answers in terms of the job for which you are being examined.

Basis of Rating

Probably you will forget most of these "do's" and "don'ts" when you walk into the oral interview room. Even remembering them all will not ensure you a passing grade. Perhaps you did not have the qualifications in the first place. But remembering them will help you to put your best foot forward, without treading on the toes of the board members.

Rumor and popular opinion to the contrary notwithstanding, an oral board wants you to make the best appearance possible. They know you are under pressure – but they also want to see how you respond to it as a guide to what your reaction would be under the pressures of the job you seek. They will be influenced by the degree of poise you display, the personal traits you show and the manner in which you respond.

ABOUT THIS BOOK

This book contains tests divided into Examination Sections. Go through each test, answering every question in the margin. We have also attached a sample answer sheet at the back of the book that can be removed and used. At the end of each test look at the answer key and check your answers. On the ones you got wrong, look at the right answer choice and learn. Do not fill in the answers first. Do not memorize the questions and answers, but understand the answer and principles involved. On your test, the questions will likely be different from the samples. Questions are changed and new ones added. If you understand these past questions you should have success with any changes that arise. Tests may consist of several types of questions. We have additional books on each subject should more study be advisable or necessary for you. Finally, the more you study, the better prepared you will be. This book is intended to be the last thing you study before you walk into the examination room. Prior study of relevant texts is also recommended. NLC publishes some of these in our Fundamental Series. Knowledge and good sense are important factors in passing your exam. Good luck also helps. So now study this Passbook, absorb the material contained within and take that knowledge into the examination. Then do your best to pass that exam.

EXAMINATION SECTION

EXAMINATION SECTION
TEST 1

DIRECTIONS: Each question or incomplete statement is followed by several suggested answers or completions. Select the one that BEST answers the question or completes the statement. *PRINT THE LETTER OF THE CORRECT ANSWER IN THE SPACE AT THE RIGHT.*

1. On the monthly report of the amount of work completed, the units used to measure the amount of work completed on guardrails and beam barriers installed on arterial highways is

    A. square feet
    B. square yards
    C. linear feet
    D. linear yards

2. On the daily work report for the sidewalk concrete gang is a formula, $M = [G - (D + U)]$, where G = total man-hours worked, D = total man-hours delays, U = total man-hours unmeasured work, and M = total man-hours measured work.
   If G = 98, D = 42, U = 21, then M is equal to

    A. 35   B. 56   C. 77   D. 119

3. When a plumber *opens a street*, he is responsible for restoring the pavement. After completion of the permanent restoration, the plumber is responsible for maintaining the restored area for a total period of

    A. six months
    B. one year
    C. one year and 6 months
    D. two years

4. A permit for a street opening may be issued for a single permit activity for one block length up to a MAXIMUM length of _____ feet.

    A. 50   B. 100   C. 200   D. 300

5. A street obstruction bond taken out by a contractor working in the street is to insure the city if

    A. a pedestrian is injured by material stored on the sidewalk
    B. an automobile is damaged by material stored in the street
    C. curbs, sidewalks, and pavements are damaged
    D. obstructions, illegally placed in the street, must be removed

6. On the daily work report for the sidewalk concrete gang is an item *curb*.
   The different types of curb listed on the report are: bluestone or granite, concrete-steel face, concrete-regular face, and

    A. drop
    B. paving block
    C. concrete block
    D. prefabricated

7. On the monthly report of work output under time (manhours) is a column headed MSO, which refers to manhours

    A. of mechanical services operator other than MVO
    B. of operation time lost while waiting
    C. of operation time lost due to the weather
    D. spent operating mechanical equipment by the MVO

8. In the city, concrete sidewalks are required to have a minimum thickness of concrete of _____ inches.

   A. 3 B. 4 C. 5 D. 6

9. Asphalt was laid for a length of 210 feet on the entire width of a street whose curb-to-curb distance is 30 feet. The number of square yards covered with asphalt is MOST NEARLY

   A. 210 B. 700 C. 2100 D. 6300

10. A layer of cinders is used as a base for a concrete sidewalk. The MAIN purpose of the cinders is to

    A. act as an air entraining agent for the concrete in the sidewalk
    B. replace poor soil under the sidewalk
    C. provide drainage under the sidewalk
    D. cushion the sidewalk when heavy loads are placed on the sidewalk

11. The unit used on the daily gang report to report the amount of measurement of debris removed is

    A. square foot   B. square yard
    C. cubic foot   D. cubic yard

12. 627 cubic feet contains MOST NEARLY _____ cubic yards.

    A. 21 B. 22 C. 23 D. 24

13. Of the following, the one that is INCORRECT curb construction is a curb made

    A. with a height of 5 inches
    B. with a steel angle for the face
    C. without a steel face
    D. monolithically with the sidewalk

14. Where feasible, concrete sidewalk panels should be made in squares of _____ feet by _____ feet.

    A. 3; 3 B. 5; 5 C. 6; 6 D. 7; 7

15. The steel facing for concrete curbs are splayed

    A. at an expansion joint
    B. where it butts against an adjacent steel plate
    C. at a drop curb
    D. at a radius bend

16. Expansion joints in steel curb facing shall be 1/4 inch wide and shall be filled with

    A. sand   B. premolded filler
    C. poured asphalt   D. dry pack

17. One inch is MOST NEARLY equal to _____ feet.

    A. 0.8 B. 0.08 C. 0.008 D. 0.0008

18. Of the following, the *final* finish on a sidewalk is MOST frequently made with a   18.____

    A. wood float   B. screed
    C. steel trowel   D. darby

19. An air entraining compound would be added to concrete MAINLY to   19.____

    A. make the concrete lighter
    B. make the concrete cure faster
    C. improve the resistance of the concrete to frost action
    D. increase the tensile strength of the concrete

20. *ASTM*, as used in specifications for concrete, is an abbreviation for the   20.____

    A. American Society for Testing Materials
    B. American Standard Training Manual
    C. American Standard Testing Materials
    D. Association of Scientists for Testing Materials

21. A 15-foot-wide sidewalk has a pitch of 1/4 inch per foot. The difference in elevation from   21.____
    the curb to 15 feet from the curb in the direction of the pitch is _____ inches.

    A. 3   B. 3 3/4   C. 4   D. 4 1/2

22. A liquid asphalt is designated *RC70*.   22.____
    The letters RC stand for

    A. Rough Course   B. Rubber Cement
    C. Rapid Curing   D. Reinforced Concrete

23. Unless otherwise specified, steel faced concrete curb shall consist of the steel curb fac-   23.____
    ing in _____-foot lengths.

    A. 5   B. 10   C. 15   D. 20

24. The difference between sheet asphalt and asphaltic concrete is that sheet asphalt   24.____

    A. contains no sand while asphaltic concrete contains sand
    B. contains no coarse aggregate while asphaltic concrete contains coarse aggregate
    C. contains no mineral filler while asphaltic concrete contains mineral filler
    D. has no flux while asphaltic concrete has flux

25. An approved roller shall weigh not less than 225 pounds per inch width of main roll.   25.____
    If the main roll width is 60 inches, the MINIMUM roller weight shall be equal to or
    greater than _____ lbs.

    A. 12,000   B. 12,500   C. 13,000   D. 13,500

KEY (CORRECT ANSWERS)

1.	C	11.	D
2.	A	12.	C
3.	D	13.	D
4.	D	14.	B
5.	C	15.	C
6.	A	16.	B
7.	A	17.	B
8.	B	18.	A
9.	B	19.	C
10.	C	20.	A

21. B
22. C
23. D
24. B
25. D

TEST 2

DIRECTIONS: Each question or incomplete statement is followed by several suggested answers or completions. Select the one that BEST answers the question or completes the statement. *PRINT THE LETTER OF THE CORRECT ANSWER IN THE SPACE AT THE RIGHT.*

1. A specification states that the rate of application of asphalt cement shall be 1 1/2 gallons per square yard with a tolerance of 1/10 of a gallon.
   Of the following, the rate of application that would be acceptable is _____ gallons per square yard.

   A. 1.2 B. 1.3 C. 1.6 D. 1.7

2. Of the following, the BEST reason for compacting backfill is to

   A. prevent settlement
   B. crush oversized rocks
   C. facilitate drainage
   D. make the soil uniform

3. Asphalt block is hexagonal tile block.
   The number of vertical sides of each block in place is

   A. 4 B. 6 C. 8 D. 10

4. Concrete driveways shall have a MINIMUM thickness of concrete of _____ inches.

   A. 5 B. 6 C. 7 D. 8

5. When the tops of manholes must be raised because of repaving, the MOST practical of the following methods to use is to

   A. break out the manhole frame and replace it with a deeper frame
   B. remove the manhole frame, build up the top of the manhole with bricks, and reset the frame
   C. use a thicker manhole cover
   D. place a metal collar on top of the existing frame

6. In a 1:2:4 concrete mix, the 2 indicates the quantity of

   A. water B. sand C. cement D. aggregate

7. A tree pit shall be located in the area immediately in back of the curb.
   The MAXIMUM size of the tree pit shall be

   A. 3' x 3' B. 4' x 4' C. 5' x 5' D. 6' x 6'

8. A temporary asphaltic pavement is placed over an excavation in the street by a private contractor.
   The MINIMUM required thickness of the finish course of the temporary asphaltic pavement is _____ inch(es).

   A. 1 B. 2 C. 3 D. 4

9. When a vault is abandoned, it must be filled in with clean incombustible materials, well-tamped.
   Where such structures adjoin the curb of a street, the roof must be removed and the enclosing walls cut down below the curb to a depth of _____ feet.

   A. 2 B. 4 C. 6 D. 8

10. Granite curbs are required to be set on a cradle. The MAIN purpose of the cradle is to

    A. prevent cracking of the curb
    B. prevent settling of the curb
    C. help keep the curb in line while it is being set
    D. separate the curb from the adjacent sidewalk

11. Paving was installed on a street from Station 3+15 to Station 4+90.
    The length of street that was paved is _____ feet.

    A. 75   B. 115   C. 175   D. 215

12. A district foreman uses an engineer's tape and measures a distance of 26.50 feet. This distance is equal to _____ feet _____ inch(es).

    A. 26; 5   B. 26; 6   C. 26; 1/2   D. 26; 0.6

13. Written on a can containing material delivered from a manufacturer is the notation *Approved by the B.S. & A.*
    The B.S. & A. is an abbreviation for the

    A. Bureau of Shipping and Allocation
    B. Board of Standards and Appeals
    C. Board of Supervision and Approval
    D. Bureau of Supervision and Assistance

14. An asphalt macadam pavement consists of a base course and a wearing course. The purpose of the base course is to

    A. provide drainage
    B. provide a level surface for the wearing course
    C. spread the load from the surface when it reaches the soil
    D. replace defective soil

15. Of the following, the MOST important recent advancement in power-driven equipment and tools is

    A. reduction in weight of the equipment
    B. improved surface finish
    C. higher operating speed
    D. lower noise levels

16. A wooden horse, used to warn traffic away, should be placed in front of which of the following defects in the street?
    A

    A. broken curb
    B. piece of roadway pavement that is very thin and the pavement whose base is starting to show through
    C. very badly broken manhole cover in the center of the street
    D. catch basin filled to the surface with debris

17. When a street is to be paved, the roller should 17.____
    A. start at the curb, go the length of the street and then move toward the center
    B. move from curb to curb transversely across the street
    C. start at the center, go the length of the street, and then move toward the curb
    D. roll at all the manhole covers first and then start rolling the length of the street

18. The use of long chutes to place concrete for a road base is usually prohibited. 18.____
    The BEST of the following reasons for prohibiting long chutes in this case is that
    A. the concrete will set by the time it is in place
    B. the water will evaporate from the mix
    C. segregation of the aggregate will occur
    D. the stone will be broken down into smaller particles

19. When sheet asphalt is spread by hand, the speed of the rolling should NOT exceed 19.____
    _____ square yards per hour.
    A. 100   B. 300   C. 500   D. 700

20. Of the following, the BEST way to insure long trouble-free operation of mechanical equipment is by periodic inspection and 20.____
    A. use   B. servicing
    C. painting   D. rotation of operators

21. Of the following maintenance work, the one type that is LEAST likely to be done by your agency on mechanical equipment is 21.____
    A. tune-up   B. repairing
    C. overhauling   D. rebuilding

22. Of the following, the MOST important equipment needed to lay sheet asphalt pavement is truck, roller, fire wagon, and 22.____
    A. grader   B. distributor
    C. planer   D. spreader

23. Of the following, the BEST reason why deep potholes should be repaired *immediately* is that 23.____
    A. they look bad
    B. they are a safety hazard
    C. they present a drainage problem
    D. people complaining about unfilled potholes cause unfavorable publicity

24. Of the following, the MOST serious safety hazard on highway and street maintenance work is 24.____
    A. injury from flying debris during pavement breaking
    B. motor traffic
    C. working close to trucks, bulldozers, and rollers
    D. cave-ins

25. Of the following, the BEST way a laborer can avoid accidents is to

    A. work slowly
    B. be alert
    C. wear safety shoes
    D. wear glasses

26. Of the following, the BEST first aid treatment for a second degree burn is to cover the burn with a _____ sterile dressing.

    A. thin, wet
    B. thin, dry
    C. thick, wet
    D. thick, dry

27. One of the laborers on the job feels unusually tired, has a headache and nausea, is perspiring heavily, and the skin is pale and clammy.
    He is probably suffering from

    A. epilepsy
    B. food poisoning
    C. heat exhaustion
    D. sunstroke

28. If a laborer feels faint, the BEST advice to give him is to advise him to

    A. lie flat with his head low
    B. walk around till he revives
    C. run around till he revives
    D. drink a glass of cold water

29. Of the following types of fire extinguisher, the one to use on an electrical fire is

    A. soda acid
    B. carbon dioxide
    C. water pump tank
    D. pyrene

30. The GREATEST number of injuries from equipment used in construction work result from

    A. carelessness of the operator
    B. poor maintenance of the equipment
    C. overloading of the equipment
    D. poor inspection of the equipment

KEY (CORRECT ANSWERS)

1.	C	16.	C
2.	A	17.	A
3.	B	18.	C
4.	C	19.	B
5.	D	20.	B
6.	B	21.	D
7.	C	22.	D
8.	C	23.	B
9.	A	24.	B
10.	B	25.	B
11.	C	26.	D
12.	B	27.	C
13.	B	28.	A
14.	C	29.	B
15.	D	30.	A

EXAMINATION SECTION
TEST 1

DIRECTIONS: Each question or incomplete statement is followed by several suggested answers or completions. Select the one that BEST answers the question or completes the statement. *PRINT THE LETTER OF THE CORRECT ANSWER IN THE SPACE AT THE RIGHT.*

1. To prevent asphalt from sticking to the inner surfaces of a dump truck, the surfaces should be sprayed with 1.____

    A. gasoline
    B. water
    C. kerosene
    D. heavy fuel oil

2. A pneumatic roller 2.____

    A. is steam powered
    B. has rubber tires
    C. has steel rolls
    D. is diesel powered

3. A trench is 4'0" wide by 8'6" deep by 48'0" long. The volume of earth removed to form this trench, in cubic yards, is MOST NEARLY 3.____

    A. 62 B. 60 C. 58 D. 56

4. The presence of lumps in a sheet asphalt mixture is MOST likely an indication that the mixture 4.____

    A. is too cold
    B. is too hot
    C. does not contain enough asphaltic cement
    D. contains too much sand

5. The bedding material for granite block pavement is usually 5.____

    A. asphalt
    B. concrete
    C. sand
    D. mineral dust

6. Cold patch asphalt is usually shipped by the manufacturer in 6.____

    A. steel drums
    B. wooden kegs
    C. cloth sacks
    D. aluminum sacks

7. The proper drainage of a street is LEAST dependent upon the _____ the street. 7.____

    A. crown of
    B. gutters of
    C. manholes in
    D. inlets of

8. The dead end of a vitrified pipe sewer should 8.____

    A. be closed with a bulkhead of brick masonry
    B. be closed with a wooden bulkhead
    C. have a cast iron gate valve
    D. be left open

9. The ONLY portions of vitrified pipe which should be left partly unglazed or scored with parallel lines are the _____ spigot. 9.____

A. *outside* of the hub and the inside of the
B. *inside* of the hub and the outside of the
C. *outside* of both hub and
D. *inside* of both hub and

10. A manhole cover which had few or no openings would MOST likely be used on a manhole built

    A. for a sanitary sewer
    B. for a combined sewer
    C. for a storm sewer
    D. under a sidewalk

11. Bituminous material is normally used to make joints in sewer pipe when the sewer is a _____ sewer _____ the normal water table.

    A. sanitary; above
    B. sanitary; alongside
    C. storm; above
    D. storm; below

12. Assume that Class A concrete is a 1:2:4 mix with 6 gallons of water per sack of cement, and Class B concrete is a 1:2 1/2:5 mix with 6 gallons of water per sack of cement.
    With reference to the foregoing, the statement MOST NEARLY correct is that the

    A. Class A concrete is much stronger
    B. Class B concrete is much stronger
    C. number of cubic feet of concrete per sack of cement is greater for the Class A concrete
    D. number of cubic feet of concrete per sack of cement is greater for the Class B concrete

13. When fresh concrete is to be placed on concrete that has already set, the one of the following procedures which would be MOST accurate is that the existing surface of concrete should be

    A. cleaned
    B. cleaned and wet down
    C. cleaned, wet down, and roughened
    D. cleaned, wet down, roughened, and coated with a grout of neat cement

14. Assume that a specification reads: Bats may be used in inside ring of arch and inverts for closers only.
    The bats referred to are usually made of

    A. concrete   B. wood   C. brick   D. metal

15. Other things being equal, close sheeting is MOST likely to be required in trenches which are

    A. shallow   B. deep   C. wide   D. narrow

16. Assume that a foreman on a trenching job insists that the road surface adjacent to the trench be swept periodically.
    It is MOST likely that his reason for doing so is PRIMARILY based on consideration of

    A. appearance
    B. safety
    C. fussiness
    D. keeping someone busy

17. The head of a bar that was used to break concrete has been redressed and tempered. This is usually

   A. *good* practice, because a mushroomed head is dangerous
   B. *bad* practice, because it should not have been tempered
   C. *good* practice, because it restores the bar to its original condition
   D. *bad* practice, because it adds to the cost of the job

18. When lifting a heavy object, a man should NOT

   A. keep his back straight and vertical
   B. place his feet wide apart
   C. bend at the knees to grasp the object
   D. get a firm hold on the object

19. Ignoring the overlap, the length, in inches, of the gasket for a gasket and mortar joint on a 12-inch (internal diameter) pipe with a wall thickness of 1 inch is MOST NEARLY

   A. 38   B. 41   C. 44   D. 47

20. The mortar that is used for a gasket and mortar joint on a vitrified pipe sewer is

   A. neat cement grout
   B. 1 part cement, 1 to 1 1/2 parts sand, mixed with water
   C. 1 part cement, 3 parts sand, mixed with water
   D. 1 part cement, 1 part sand, 1 part gravel, mixed with water

21. The MOST important function performed by the gasket in a gasket and mortar joint is to

   A. keep the mortar out of the pipe
   B. reduce the quantity of mortar used
   C. keep the spigot centered in the hub
   D. provide a cushion when the mortar is being rammed

22. The length of a single section of sewer rod that is used for cleaning is usually limited by

   A. weight considerations
   B. the strength of the material used for the rod
   C. the size of manhole cover
   D. the diameter of manhole at sewer elevation

23. Aside from safety considerations, the MOST important function of close sheeting in trenching is to

   A. prevent undermining of adjacent pavement
   B. improve the appearance of the job
   C. make it easier to use excavating machinery
   D. keep out water

24. Assume that a pump is being used to pump out a deep cellar which has been flooded. Of the following distances, the one which will MOST likely prevent the operation of the pump if the distance is too large is the

A. vertical distance between pump and inlet
B. horizontal distance between pump and inlet
C. sloping distance between pump and inlet
D. horizontal distance from pump to outlet

25. A change in the slope of a vitrified pipe sewer should be located 25.____

    A. a few feet upstream from a manhole
    B. a few feet downstream from a manhole
    C. midway between manholes
    D. at a manhole

KEY (CORRECT ANSWERS)

1.	C	11.	A
2.	B	12.	D
3.	B	13.	D
4.	A	14.	C
5.	C	15.	B
6.	A	16.	B
7.	C	17.	B
8.	A	18.	B
9.	B	19.	C
10.	D	20.	B

21. C
22. D
23. A
24. A
25. D

TEST 2

DIRECTIONS: Each question or incomplete statement is followed by several suggested answers or completions. Select the one that BEST answers the question or completes the statement. *PRINT THE LETTER OF THE CORRECT ANSWER IN THE SPACE AT THE RIGHT.*

1. Box sheeting differs from regular sheeting PRIMARILY in   1.____

    A. size of timber used for sheeting
    B. that it is used in trenches of short length
    C. that it is used in trenches of greater width
    D. the direction in which the sheeting is placed

2. Assume that sewage is flowing out of three adjacent manholes on a sewer line.   2.____
   It is MOST logical to expect that there is an obstruction

    A. between the center manhole and the higher one
    B. between the center manhole and the lower one
    C. anywhere between the three manholes
    D. outside the stretch of sewer between the three manholes

3. Earth used to backfill a vitrified pipe sewer trench   3.____

    A. should not contain any stones
    B. may contain stones if the stones are less than 10 inches in largest dimension
    C. should contain only those stones removed from the trench
    D. may contain stones up to 10 inches in largest dimension provided there are no stones in the backfill which is within 2 feet of the pipe

4. When laying bell and spigot sewer pipe, it is GOOD practice to place the ball end   4.____

    A. away from the outlet
    B. toward the outlet
    C. either way
    D. away from the outlet when the sewer has a flat slope

5. The number of board feet in 22 pieces of 2 x 6's, 12'6" long is MOST NEARLY   5.____

    A. 275   B. 270   C. 265   D. 260

6. A riser would MOST likely be used on a _____ sewer.   6.____

    A. shallow   B. vitrified pipe
    C. deep   D. reinforced concrete pipe

7. If, after ramming, a granite block is found to be too low, it should be   7.____

    A. replaced with a thicker block
    B. removed with a pinch bar
    C. covered with mortar
    D. removed with tongs

8. A separating agent, such as calcium chloride, would MOST likely be used on a(n)   8.____
   _____ pavement with _____ filler.

15

A. granite block; cement grout
B. asphalt block; cement grout joint
C. granite block; asphaltic joint
D. poured concrete; cement grout joint

9. Assume that granite block has been redressed.
   The dimension which is MOST likely to be the same as that on the original block is

   A. length   B. width   C. depth   D. none

10. Spacing strips are MOST likely to be used when laying _____ block pavement with _____ joint filler.

    A. asphalt; cement grout
    B. asphalt; asphaltic
    C. granite; cement grout
    D. granite; asphaltic

11. The piece of equipment MOST likely to be used both for sheet asphalt pavement and asphalt block pavement is a(n)

    A. tamper
    B. smoothing iron
    C. asphalt rake
    D. asphalt kettle

12. In cleaning a steel reinforcing bar for reinforced concrete, it is LEAST important to remove

    A. rust   B. grease   C. oil   D. paint

13. Concrete that is used for a concrete base for pavement should have a slump of MOST NEARLY _____ inches.

    A. 10   B. 8   C. 6   D. 3

14. A concrete mix can be made more workable without reducing its strength by adding to the mix

    A. cement
    B. water
    C. cement and water
    D. coarse aggregate

15. Forms for concrete are usually oiled to

    A. prevent honeycombing
    B. make the form watertight
    C. prevent segregation
    D. make stripping easier

16. The backlash in a roller used on sheet asphalt is

    A. *good,* because it makes for faster operation
    B. *good,* because it makes the operator's job easier
    C. *bad,* because it results in waves in the asphalt
    D. *bad,* because it requires more asphaltic cement

17. The LARGEST particles in the binder course of a sheet asphalt pavement usually consists of

    A. broken stone
    B. sand
    C. smooth round pebbles
    D. rock dust

18. It is important to remove water which has seeped into bell holes in a sewer trench because

    A. this makes the caulker more comfortable
    B. this water will spoil the joint
    C. this water will preserve the stability of the trench bottom
    D. the water is unsanitary

19. Of the following materials, the one which would be MOST combustible is _____ asphalt.

    A. RG cutback   B. MC cutback
    C. SC cutback   D. emulsified

20. The one and one-half inch stones of a base for an asphalt macadam pavement have been rolled.
    The BEST time to apply the asphalt cement is

    A. immediately after the rolling
    B. after the rolled stones have been wet down with water
    C. after sand has been spread over the broken stone
    D. after sand has been spread and rolled

21. The binder course of a sheet asphalt pavement has been laid today. The surface course should be placed

    A. today   B. tomorrow
    C. the day after tomorrow   D. any day next week

Questions 22-23.

DIRECTIONS: Questions 22 and 23 refer to a 12-inch sewer line which is being constructed without a cradle in a clay soil.

22. Before the pipe is placed in the trench, the bottom of the trench should be excavated to a depth of MOST NEARLY _____ inches _____ the invert.

    A. 12; below   B. 6; below
    C. 12; above   D. 6; above

23. After the pipe is properly bedded, the excavated material should be replaced in layers

    A. 6 inches thick, each layer being flooded with water
    B. 6 inches thick, each layer being tamped
    C. 4 feet thick, each layer being tamped
    D. 2 feet thick, each layer being flooded with water

24. In sewer work, pargeting would MOST likely be required on

    A. vitrified pipe sewers
    B. manholes
    C. cast iron pipe sewers
    D. reinforced concrete pipe sewers

25. A seal coat for an asphalt macadam base course has been applied by a pressure distrib- 25. ____
utor.
Before a seal coat is rolled, it should be

    A. allowed to cool
    B. covered with broken stone
    C. wet down with water
    D. squeegeed over the surface

KEY (CORRECT ANSWERS)

1.	D	11.	D
2.	D	12.	A
3.	D	13.	D
4.	A	14.	C
5.	A	15.	D
6.	C	16.	C
7.	D	17.	A
8.	C	18.	B
9.	C	19.	A
10.	A	20.	A

21. A
22. B
23. B
24. B
25. B

EXAMINATION SECTION
TEST 1

DIRECTIONS: Each question consists of a statement. You are to indicate whether the statement is TRUE (T) or FALSE (F). *PRINT THE LETTER OF THE CORRECT ANSWER IN THE SPACE AT THE RIGHT.*

1. A stillson wrench may properly be used on wrought iron pipe. 1.____

2. A pneumatic hammer is run by electricity. 2.____

3. A pneumatic drill, when not in use, should be left standing on its rod. 3.____

4. A cubic yard contains 27 cubic feet. 4.____

5. A tarpaulin is a lubricating oil for air compressors. 5.____

6. In working in manholes or pits, it is advisable to have one or two of the crew outside in case of emergency. 6.____

7. Men should be cautioned against entering manholes or vaults without first testing the air inside. 7.____

8. An air compressor is best used to yarn a joint. 8.____

9. To dig a trench, it is best to use a square-pointed shovel. 9.____

10. A street or road which rises at a uniform grade of 5 feet in 100 feet has a 5% grade. 10.____

11. If a candle will burn at the bottom of a manhole, it is a sign of gas and men should keep out. 11.____

12. It is good practice to wait until a sewer has been ventilated before going down into it. 12.____

13. It is good practice to drop lighted matches down a manhole to see if gas is present. 13.____

14. Workmen handling tar or asphalt should have their trousers fastened tightly around their ankles. 14.____

15. Cement brought to a job in bags should be piled neatly in criss-cross stacks on the ground. 15.____

16. Bagged cement should be piled about 25 bags high. 16.____

17. Men placing cement and concrete should have sleeves rolled up since they can work faster that way. 17.____

18. When mixing concrete, workmen should not stand so the wind blows in their faces. 18.____

19. Manholes are provided at suitable intervals along a sewer so that it may be inspected and cleaned. 19.____

20. The operator of a pneumatic drill should grasp it very loosely to prevent fatigue from constant vibration. 20.____

21. A catch basin's main use is to prevent storm water from entering a combined sewer. 21.____

22. Catch basins are generally built of brick or concrete. 22.____

23. Catch basins in New York City are generally cleaned by the use of orange peel type buckets. 23.____

24. A flexible rod is a tool often used in cleaning sewers. 24.____

25. Sewer obstructions can be removed by running scrapers and brushes through the sewer pipe. 25.____

KEY (CORRECT ANSWERS)

1.	T	11.	F
2.	F	12.	T
3.	F	13.	F
4.	T	14.	T
5.	F	15.	F
6.	T	16.	F
7.	T	17.	F
8.	F	18.	T
9.	F	19.	T
10.	T	20.	F

21. F
22. T
23. T
24. T
25. T

TEST 2

DIRECTIONS: Each question consists of a statement. You are to indicate whether the statement is TRUE (T) or FALSE (F). *PRINT THE LETTER OF THE CORRECT ANSWER IN THE SPACE AT THE RIGHT.*

1. In flushing sewers, the amount of water used is more important than the speed at which the water is played into the sewer. 1.____
2. Many pavement failures can be traced to the action of water or moisture. 2.____
3. A pot hole in paving is a device for heating tar. 3.____
4. A surface heater is usually used to heat the binder course. 4.____
5. Tampers are used to compact a pavement in places where rollers cannot reach. 5.____
6. A straight edge is used to determine the smoothness of a finished pavement. 6.____
7. Concrete is a mixture of cement, sand, gravel and water in the proper proportions. 7.____
8. To clean a concrete mixer, you should operate it with water and small stones in the drum. 8.____
9. A concrete mixture will do a satisfactory job if it is allowed to stand one hour before placing. 9.____
10. Rapid drying of concrete adds to its strength. 10.____
11. In mixing concrete, the quantity of water used makes no difference. 11.____
12. Cracks in concrete open wider in cold weather. 12.____
13. A 1:2:4 concrete mix means one part cement, two parts sand, and four parts gravel. 13.____
14. Coarse aggregate consists of clean crushed rock or gravel. 14.____
15. A good way to prevent concrete from sticking to forms is to wet the forms with oil. 15.____
16. Concrete that has partly set in the mixer can be broken up and used with another batch of concrete. 16.____
17. Wings of a roadway are at the same elevation as center line. 17.____
18. The crown of a street is the fall from the center to edges. 18.____
19. A cold patch mixture when ready to be deposited usually contains wire mesh. 19.____
20. Grout is used to fill cracks in asphalt pavement. 20.____
21. In pouring cracks, just enough material should be used to fill the opening. 21.____
22. In hot weather, a pavement will contract. 22.____
23. Streets should usually be patched with the same material used in their construction. 23.____

24. Expansion joints are used in paving to provide for changes in temperature. 24.____

25. The main purpose of a seal coat in paving is to water-proof a surface. 25.____

KEY (CORRECT ANSWERS)

1. F
2. T
3. F
4. F
5. T

6. T
7. T
8. T
9. F
10. F

11. F
12. T
13. T
14. T
15. T

16. F
17. F
18. T
19. F
20. F

21. T
22. F
23. T
24. T
25. T

EXAMINATION SECTION
TEST 1

DIRECTIONS: Each question or incomplete statement is followed by several suggested answers or completions. Select the one that BEST answers the question or completes the statement. *PRINT THE LETTER OF THE CORRECT ANSWER IN THE SPACE AT THE RIGHT.*

1. Of the following statements relating to new bell and spigot pipe being laid in a trench, the one that is CORRECT is that

    A. the enlarged end of the pipe faces downstream
    B. bell and spigot pipe is usually elliptical in shape
    C. when building a new line using bell and spigot pipe, you start from the downstream end
    D. vitrified pipe is usually thicker than concrete pipe of the same diameter

2. Vitrified pipe is made of

    A. clay   B. vermiculite
    C. gypsum   D. Portland cement

3. The invert of a sewer pipe is its

    A. outer top   B. inner bottom
    C. inner top   D. outer bottom

4. A cradle is usually placed under a sewer pipe when the

    A. trench is narrow   B. trench is wide
    C. soil is poor   D. pipe is near the surface

5. A monolithic sewer is a

    A. vitrified pipe sewer
    B. sewer carrying only storm water
    C. cast-iron sewer containing bell and spigot joints
    D. reinforced concrete cast-in-place sewer

6. Of the following, the BEST reason for placing manholes on sewers is to

    A. provide access for inspection and maintenance
    B. allow for overflow during a heavy storm
    C. pinpoint the location of the sewer
    D. give access to the sewer for the purpose of snow removal

7. The sheeting in a trench for a sheeted sewer is ordered left in place after the sewer has been built and backfilled. The BEST reason for ordering the sheeting left in place is that

    A. the sheeting is too expensive to remove
    B. the removal of the sheeting would disturb the sewer
    C. this minimizes the settlement outside the sheeted area
    D. the sheeting is too difficult to remove

8. The two MOST frequently used types of sheeting for normal soil conditions and average depths are

   A. soldier beams with horizontal sheeting and vertical wood sheeting with bracing
   B. steel sheet piling and vertical wood sheeting
   C. precast concrete planks with soldier beams and steel sheet piling
   D. slurry walls and vertical wood sheeting

9. A specification for a new sewer requires that the pavement NOT be restored for a period of at least six months after the backfill is in place.
   The BEST reason for this requirement is to

   A. be sure that the sewer will work before restoring the pavement
   B. minimize the settlement of the pavement
   C. defer final payment to the contractor
   D. allow the use of a lighter pavement

10. In reinforced concrete sewers, the reinforcing steel must have a minimum cover of concrete.
    Of the following, the BEST reason for this requirement is to

    A. make the sewer watertight
    B. protect the reinforcing steel against corrosion
    C. allow the use of smaller sized stone in the concrete
    D. eliminate the need for vibrating concrete

11. As used in relation to sewers, infiltration refers to the

    A. leakage of sewage from the sewer to the surrounding soil
    B. connection of sanitary sewer lines into storm water sewers
    C. inflow of ground water into the sewer
    D. loss of mortar at the joints of prefabricated sewers

12. A BAD effect of infiltration in a sanitary sewer is that it

    A. tends to overload the sewage treatment plant
    B. corrodes the sewer
    C. causes cavitation in the sewer
    D. increases the carrying capacity of the sewer

13. A storm sewer GENERALLY differs from a sanitary sewer in that a storm sewer

    A. is generally larger in size than a sanitary sewer and carries little dry-weather flow
    B. is generally made of concrete whereas a sanitary sewer is generally made of cast iron
    C. generally requires fewer manholes than a sanitary sewer
    D. generally has a large slope whereas a sanitary sewer generally has a small slope

14. Manhole frames and covers are USUALLY made of

    A. aluminum   B. malleable iron
    C. cast iron   D. steel

15. The spacing of rungs used for steps in a manhole is MOST NEARLY _____ inches. 15.____
    A. 4 B. 12 C. 20 D. 26

16. Steel is galvanized by coating it with 16.____
    A. tin B. lead C. copper D. zinc

17. The reinforcing steel in a cast-in-place concrete sewer section would MOST likely be placed as shown in 17.____

    A.   B.

    C.   D.

18. Well points would MOST likely be used in the construction of a sewer when the 18.____
    A. sewer is very deep
    B. sewer is in rock
    C. soil is clayey
    D. water table is above the sewer

19. The purpose of jetting the well points in sewer construc-tion is to 19.____
    A. clean out the screen
    B. set the well point in place
    C. clean out the area outside the screen
    D. remove water from the surrounding area

20. The type of soil in which well points operate MOST efficiently is 20.____
    A. sand B. clay C. rock D. silt

21. The water-cement ratio of a concrete mix is USUALLY expressed in terms of 21.____
    A. barrels of cement per gallon of water
    B. bags of cement per gallon of water
    C. gallons of water per bag of cement
    D. gallons of water per barrel of cement

22. The effective diameter of a number 4 reinforcing bar is MOST NEARLY _____ inch.
    A. 1/4   B. 1/2   C. 3/4   D. 1

23. The PRIMARY purpose of curing freshly poured concrete is to
    A. keep the surface smooth
    B. prevent honeycombing of the surface
    C. improve the appearance of the surface
    D. prevent evaporation of water from the surface

24. A bag of cement weighs MOST NEARLY _____ pounds.
    A. 94   B. 104   C. 114   D. 124

25. Of the following, the material that may be used as the coarse aggregate in ordinary Portland cement concrete is
    A. well graded sand
    B. sand of uniform size
    C. crushed rock
    D. micaschist

26. In a 1:2:4 concrete mix, the 2 stands for the quantity of
    A. water
    B. fine aggregate
    C. coarse aggregate
    D. cement

27. The height of a slump cone used in concrete testing is _____ inches.
    A. 6   B. 8   C. 10   D. 12

28. As commonly used, 3000-pound concrete refers to 3000 pounds per
    A. inch
    B. square inch
    C. cubic inch
    D. foot

29. The factor that has the GREATEST effect on the strength of concrete is the
    A. size of coarse aggregate
    B. uniformity of the aggregate
    C. water-cement ratio
    D. quality of the fine aggregate

30. The number of bags of cement needed to produce a cubic yard of concrete is called the _____ factor.
    A. cement   B. yield   C. bulk   D. output

31. The MAIN purpose of vibrating newly poured concrete when it is in the forms is to
    A. remove high points on the surface
    B. eliminate air pockets on the surface
    C. remove excess water
    D. distribute the aggregate evenly in the concrete

32. A cubic foot of ordinary Portland cement concrete weighs MOST NEARLY _____ pounds.
    A. 145   B. 165   C. 195   D. 220

33. The MAIN purpose of adding an air entraining agent to a concrete mix used for sidewalks is to 33.____

    A. improve the resistance of the concrete to freezing and thawing conditions
    B. decrease the weight of the concrete to lighten the dead load of the concrete
    C. increase the compressive strength of the concrete
    D. decrease the resistance of the concrete to bleeding

34. Of the following operations on a fresh concrete surface, the one that should be performed FIRST is 34.____

    A. screeding   B. floating
    C. trowelling   D. brooming

35. When concrete is referred to as *3000-pound concrete,* the *3000* refers to its strength at the end of _____ days. 35.____

    A. 7   B. 14   C. 21   D. 28

KEY (CORRECT ANSWERS)

1.	C	16.	D
2.	A	17.	A
3.	B	18.	D
4.	C	19.	B
5.	D	20.	A
6.	A	21.	C
7.	C	22.	B
8.	A	23.	D
9.	B	24.	A
10.	B	25.	C
11.	C	26.	B
12.	A	27.	D
13.	A	28.	B
14.	C	29.	C
15.	B	30.	A

31. B
32. A
33. A
34. A
35. D

TEST 2

DIRECTIONS: Each question or incomplete statement is followed by several suggested answers or completions. Select the one that BEST answers the question or completes the statement. *PRINT THE LETTER OF THE CORRECT ANSWER IN THE SPACE AT THE RIGHT.*

1. If a batch of concrete is very stiff, its MAIN characteristic is that it 1.____
   A. has a low slump B. has a high slump
   C. is undersanded D. is oversanded

2. Reinforcing steel should have the GREATEST cover of concrete when the concrete surface is 2.____
   A. in contact with the ground
   B. in contact with outside air
   C. an interior wall
   D. an interior ceiling

3. The MAIN difference between reinforced concrete and plain concrete is that plain concrete uses _____ for reinforcing. 3.____
   A. larger aggregate
   B. high early strength cement
   C. steel
   D. a low water-cement ratio

4. Of the following types of wood, the one that would MOST likely be used in form work for concrete is 4.____
   A. oak B. maple C. fir D. birch

5. The size that SEPARATES the fine aggregate from the coarse aggregate in a concrete mix is _____ inch. 5.____
   A. 1/8 B. 1/4 C. 3/8 D. 1/2

6. The MINIMUM thickness of sidewalk pavements for pedes-trian use should be _____ inches. 6.____
   A. 4 B. 5 C. 6 D. 7

7. An ADVANTAGE of using sand instead of salt on concrete roadway surfaces when snow and ice settle on them is that sand 7.____
   A. is easier to remove than salt when the snow disappears
   B. will harm catch basins less than salt when the materials are washed into the catch basin
   C. will not harm the concrete surface whereas salt is harmful to the surface
   D. will help melt the surface ice whereas salt will have no effect on the ice on the surface

8. Sidewalks should be pitched toward the street at a MINIMUM of _____ inch per _____.

   A. 1/8; foot
   B. 1/8; yard
   C. 5/8; foot
   D. 1; foot

9. A freshly poured concrete sidewalk is usually finished with a

   A. screed
   B. wood float
   C. steel trowel
   D. darby

10.

   The shape of the roadway section shown above is USUALLY a(n)

   A. circle
   B. ellipse
   C. parabola
   D. hyperbola

11. The MAIN advantage of using large coarse aggregate in a concrete mix is that

   A. the mix is more workable
   B. the mix is stronger
   C. there is a saving in cement
   D. less water is required

12. In building a new street, sidewalk, and curb in a previously unpaved area, the order of construction practically ALWAYS followed is that the

   A. sidewalk precedes the road pavement
   B. sidewalk follows the road pavement
   C. curb precedes the road pavement
   D. road pavement precedes the curb

13. The USUAL range of depth of a curb from top surface of road at curb to top of curb is _____ inches to _____ inches.

   A. 4; 8
   B. 8; 12
   C. 12; 16
   D. 16; 20

14. The dimensions of common brick are GENERALLY

   A. 2 1/4" x 2 3/4" x 12"
   B. 2 1/4" x 3 3/4" x 8"
   C. 2 3/4" x 3 3/4" x 8"
   D. 2 3/4" x 4 3/4" x 12"

15. Common brick is made of

   A. limestone
   B. sand
   C. clay
   D. loess

16. Carbon black is added to concrete to

   A. give the concrete a black color
   B. accelerate the setting of the concrete
   C. retard the setting of the concrete
   D. improve the workability of the concrete

17. When steel curb angles are used for curbs, anchors are attached, to the curb angles. The MAIN purpose of the anchors is to

    A. hold the curb in place when the curb is being poured
    B. bond the curb angle into the concrete curb
    C. anchor the curb angle into the soil
    D. anchor the curb angle into the sidewalk

17.____

18. Wire mesh is specified in pounds per

    A. square foot
    B. square yard
    C. hundred square feet
    D. hundred square yards

18.____

19.

    An asphalt pavement consists of three layers.
    The layer marked E in the sketch above is the _____ course.

    A. tack   B. binder   C. base   D. wearing

19.____

20. The BASE course of a sheet asphalt pavement is usually made of

    A. sheet asphalt
    B. concrete
    C. tar
    D. bituminous binder

20.____

21. In asphalt paving, the tack coat is USUALLY applied

    A. on the finished wearing surface
    B. on the surface of the soil to receive the pavement
    C. on hard dense impervious surfaces
    D. along the curb

21.____

22. The specification for a pavement states that the penetration of asphalt is measured in units of mm.
    This stands for

    A. micrometer
    B. macrometer
    C. manometer
    D. millimeter

22.____

23. In an asphalt pavement, the LIQUID part of the asphalt mix is

    A. bitumen   B. water   C. gasoline   D. benzene

23.____

24. The terms liquid limit, plastic limit, and plasticity index refer to tests on

    A. asphalt   B. soil   C. concrete   D. gravel

24.____

25. For a bituminous paving material, sieves and sieve analysis are used to analyze the

    A. cement   B. aggregate   C. clay   D. silt

25.____

26. The size of sidewalk panels is USUALLY

    A. 2' x 2'   B. 3' x 3'   C. 5' x 5'   D. 6' x 6'

26.____

27. The slope of a sidewalk is designated as 2 inches in 5 feet.
The drop in elevation of the sidewalk in 30' is _____ foot.

    A. one   B. 1/2 of a   C. 3/4 of a   D. 1/4 of a

28. In placing temporary asphaltic pavement upon completion of the backfill in a street opening, a 3 inch thick pavement should be laid one inch above the adjoining asphalt permanent pavement.
The MAIN reason for making the temporary pavement one inch above the finished pavement is to

    A. provide adequate drainage
    B. allow for settlement
    C. identify the temporarily paved area
    D. save excavation when the permanent pavement is placed

29. A maintenance bond for a roadway pavement is in an amount of 10% of the estimated cost.
If the estimated cost is $80,000, the maintenance bond is

    A. $80   B. $800   C. $8,000   D. $80,000

30. Specifications require that a core be taken every 700 square yards of paved roadway or fraction thereof.
A 100 foot by 200 foot rectangular area would require _____ core(s).

    A. 1   B. 2   C. 3   D. 4

31. An applicant must file a map at a scale of 1" = 40'.
Six inches on the map represents _____ feet on the ground.

    A. 600   B. 240   C. 120   D. D, 60

32. A 100' x 110' lot has an area of MOST NEARLY _____ acre.

    A. 1/8   B. 1/4   C. 3/8   D. 1/2

33. 1 inch is MOST NEARLY equal to _____ feet.

    A. .02   B. .04   C. .06   D. .08

34. The area of the triangle EFG shown at the right is MOST NEARLY _____ sq.ft.
    A. 36
    B. 42
    C. 48
    D. 54

35. Specifications state: As further security for the faith-ful performance of this contract, the comptroller shall deduct, and retain until the final payment, 10% of the value of the work certified for payment in each partial payment voucher, until the amount so deducted and retained shall equal 5% of the contract price or in the case of a unit price contract, 5% of the estimated amount to be paid to the contractor under the contract.
For a $300,000 contract, the amount to be retained at the end of the contract is

    A. $5,000   B. $10,000   C. $15,000   D. $20,000

KEY (CORRECT ANSWERS)

1.	A	16.	A
2.	A	17.	B
3.	A	18.	C
4.	C	19.	B
5.	B	20.	B
6.	A	21.	C
7.	C	22.	D
8.	A	23.	A
9.	B	24.	B
10.	C	25.	B
11.	C	26.	C
12.	C	27.	A
13.	A	28.	B
14.	B	29.	C
15.	C	30.	D

31. B
32. B
33. D
34. A
35. C

TEST 3

DIRECTIONS: Each question or incomplete statement is followed by several suggested answers or completions. Select the one that BEST answers the question or completes the statement. *PRINT THE LETTER OF THE CORRECT ANSWER IN THE SPACE AT THE RIGHT.*

Questions 1-4.

DIRECTIONS: Questions 1 through 4, inclusive, refer to the plan of a sewer shown below.

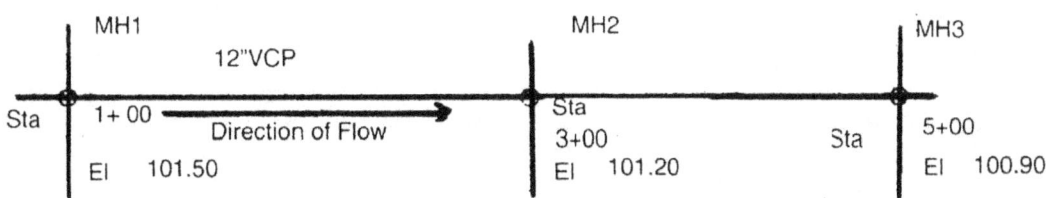

PLAN - SEWER

1. The distance, in feet, between MH1 and MH3 is _____ feet.

   A. 200   B. 300   C. 400   D. 500

2. The drop in elevation between MH1 and MH3 is

   A. 0.60'   B. 0.50'   C. 0.40'   D. 0.30'

3. If the scale of the drawing is 1 inch = 40 feet, the length of the line on the plan between MH1 and MH2 should be, in inches,

   A. 3   B. 4   C. 5   D. 6

4. A vertical section taken along the length of the sewer would be called a

   A. cross section   B. development
   C. partial plan   D. profile

5. A line joining points of equal elevation on a plan is known as a(n)

   A. profile   B. contour   C. elevation   D. isobar

6. The Federal agency concerned with safety on a construction site is

   A. OSHA   B. FIDC   C. FEMA   D. NHOC

7. A Federal safety requirement on construction sites is that

   A. a nurse must be present at all times
   B. a safety inspector, whose only duty is safety, be assigned full time to construction sites
   C. safety hats must be worn
   D. metal scaffolds are not permitted on the job site

8. Safety shoes are shoes that have a(n)

   A. extra heavy sole
   B. extra heavy heel
   C. metal covering the toe
   D. special leather covering over the ankles

9. A material whose use has been curtailed in building and heavy construction is

   A. poured cut asphalt
   B. lightweight concrete aggregate
   C. latex paint
   D. sprayed-on asbestos

10. In making a field report, it is POOR practice to erase information on the report in order to make a change because

    A. there is a question of what was changed and why it was changed
    B. you are liable to erase through the paper and tear the report
    C. the report will no longer look neat and presentable
    D. the duplicate copies will be smudged

11. It is PREFERABLE to print information on a field report rather than write it out longhand mainly because

    A. printing takes less time to write than writing long-hand
    B. printing is usually easier to read than longhand writing
    C. longhand writing on field reports is not acceptable in court cases
    D. printing occupies less space on a report than long hand writing

12. Where the length of roadway pavement is less than 100 lineal feet, the requirement of cores may be <u>waived</u>.
    The term <u>waived</u> in the above statement means MOST NEARLY

    A. eliminated   B. enforced
    C. considered   D. postponed

13. Inspectors are provided with standardized forms, and they have to fill in information as requested on the form.
    Of the following, the MAIN advantage of this type of form is that

    A. the inspector will be less likely to omit important information
    B. it is cheap to print
    C. it is confidential and only authorized people will see it
    D. it is easy to make copies of the form

14. Where only part of the sidewalk is to be relaid, the concrete shall match the <u>predominant</u> color of the existing sidewalk.
    The word <u>predominant</u> in the above sentence means MOST NEARLY

    A. lightest   B. darkest
    C. main   D. contrasting

15. All stands must be substantially built so as not to create any hazard to passersby or other persons.
The word hazard in the above sentence means MOST NEARLY

    A. delay
    B. danger
    C. obstruction
    D. inconvenience

16. The lights shall be lighted and remain lighted every night during the hours prescribed for public street lamps.
The word prescribed in the above sentence means MOST NEARLY

    A. required
    B. not needed
    C. before midnight
    D. of darkness

17. The Department of Highways in its discretion may direct that certain regulations be waived.
In the above sentence, the word discretion means MOST NEARLY

    A. jurisdiction
    B. operation
    C. organization
    D. judgment

18. A sidewalk that abuts a curb _____ the curb.

    A. is above
    B. is below
    C. touches
    D. is integral with

19. All canopy permits shall be posted in a conspicuous place at the entrance for which the permit is issued.
The word conspicuous means MOST NEARLY

    A. well known
    B. inaccessible
    C. easily observed
    D. obscure

20. Where a street opening is made by a licensed plumber, a plunber's bond may be filed in lieu of a street obstruction bond.
The words in lieu of mean MOST NEARLY

    A. in addition to
    B. instead of
    C. immediately as
    D. appurtenant to

21. Of the following characteristics of a written report, the one that is MOST important is its

    A. length
    B. accuracy
    C. organization
    D. grammar

22. A written report to your superior contains many spelling errors.
Of the following statements relating to spelling errors, the one that is MOST NEARLY correct is that

    A. this is unimportant as long as the meaning of the report is clear
    B. readers of the report will ignore the many spelling errors
    C. readers of the report will get a poor opinion of the writer of the report
    D. spelling errors are unimportant as long as the grammar is correct

23. Written reports to your superior should have the same general arrangement and layout. The BEST reason for this requirement is that the

    A. report will be more accurate
    B. report will be more complete
    C. person who reads the report will know what the subject of the report is
    D. person who reads the report will know where to look for information in the report

24. The first paragraph of a report usually contains detailed information on the subject of the report.
    Of the following, the BEST reason for this requirement is to enable the

    A. reader to quickly find the subject of the report
    B. typist to immediately determine the subject of the report so that she will understand what she is typing
    C. clerk to determine to whom copies of the report shall be routed
    D. typist to quickly determine how many copies of the report will be needed

Questions 25-26.

DIRECTIONS: Questions 25 and 26 refer to the girder shown in the sketch below.

25. A report speaks of stiffeners on girders.
    The stiffener would be the part shown as

    A. A   B. B   C. C   D. D

26. The flange would be the part shown as

    A. E   B. B   C. C   D. D

27. When an inspector is writing a report about a problem your agency handles, the report should contain four major parts: a description of the problem, the location, the details of the problem, and

    A. your recommendation
    B. references to the drawings that pertain to the problem
    C. the borough in which the problem is located
    D. the agency to whom the problem should be referred

28. A report refers to a Pratt truss.
    The material composition of the truss is MOST likely

    A. wood   B. concrete   C. steel   D. aluminum

29. A plumb bob is USUALLY used to 29.____

   A. check grades
   B. establish a vertical line
   C. hold down equipment
   D. check the grading of sand

30. As a general rule, any time a measurement is made in the field, the number of quantity 30.____
    should be immediately recorded.
    Of the following, the BEST reason for immediately recording this information is that

   A. the office is interested in receiving this information as quickly as possible
   B. this enables the inspector to complete his report more quickly
   C. this information may be needed for computations
   D. it is easy to forget or mistake numbers if they are not immediately recorded

KEY(CORRECT ANSWERS)

1.	C	16.	A
2.	A	17.	D
3.	C	18.	C
4.	D	19.	C
5.	B	20.	B
6.	A	21.	B
7.	C	22.	C
8.	C	23.	D
9.	D	24.	A
10.	A	25.	D
11.	B	26.	B
12.	A	27.	A
13.	A	28.	C
14.	C	29.	B
15.	B	30.	D

EXAMINATION SECTION
TEST 1

DIRECTIONS: Each question or incomplete statement is followed by several suggested answers or completions. Select the one that BEST answers the question or completes the statement. *PRINT THE LETTER OF THE CORRECT ANSWER IN THE SPACE AT THE RIGHT.*

1. Asphalt is derived mainly

    A. as a byproduct from the production of coke
    B. from asphalt deposits seeping to the surface of the earth
    C. from the refining of crude oil
    D. from bituminous coal

2. Cutback liquid asphalts are prepared by blending asphalt with a volatile solvent. The one of the following that is NOT used as an asphalt solvent is

    A. naphtha   B. gasoline   C. kerosene   D. toluene

3. The primary purpose of the solvent in cutback asphalt is to allow the

    A. use of a larger size aggregate in the mix
    B. application of the asphalt at a relatively low temperature
    C. application of asphalt in wet weather
    D. application of asphalt in hot weather

4. The thickness of the sheet asphalt on a sheet asphalt pavement is usually _____ inch(es).

    A. 1/2 inch to 3/4   B. 1 inch to 1 1/2
    C. 1 5/8 inches to 2   D. 2 1/4 inches to 3

5. The grade of an asphalt cement is designated as AR4000. The AR is an abbreviation for

    A. asphalt rating   B. acid resistance
    C. aged residue   D. aging resistance

6. An asphaltic emulsion is a suspension of asphalt in

    A. kerosene   B. gasoline   C. toluene   D. water

7. A very light application of asphalt on an existing paved surface will promote bond between this surface and the subsequent course is known as a(n) _____ coat.

    A. prime   B. adhesion
    C. tack   D. penetrating

8. Of the following, payment is usually made for asphalt pavements at the contract price per

    A. square inch   B. square foot
    C. square yard   D. 100 square feet

39

9. The grade of an asphalt cement is designated AR4000. The 4000 is a measure of

   A. strength   B. viscosity   C. ductility   D. density

10. Of the following, the geometric shape of a horizontal curve on a highway is

    A. parabolic
    B. hyperbolic
    C. circular
    D. elliptical

11. A borrow pit in highway construction is used

    A. for storing stormwater in a heavy rain
    B. for coarse aggregate in Portland cement concrete
    C. for coarse aggregate in asphalt concrete
    D. to obtain fill for embankments

12. Overhaul in highway construction is usually measured and paid for by the

    A. yard - cubic foot
    B. yard - cubic yard
    C. station - cubic foot
    D. station - cubic yard

13. A Benkelman beam is used in highway work

    A. as an indicator of the ability of a pavement to withstand loading
    B. to measure the roughness of an asphalt concrete pavement
    C. to measure the uniformity of an asphalt concrete pavement
    D. to measure the ability of an asphalt concrete pavement to remain serviceable if the subgrade is undermined

14. When surfacing over an existing pavement, of the following, the MOST practical way to insure that the required thickness of new pavement is met is

    A. expansion of clay when exposed to water
    B. expansion of soil when excavated
    C. waviness in a soil embankment when being compacted with a roller
    D. expansion of loamy soil when exposed to water

15. When surfacing over an existing pavement, of the following, the MOST practical way to insure that the required thickness of new pavement is met is

    A. have wood blocks of the thickness of the new pavement temporarily placed on the existing pavement to insure that the thickness requirements will be met at the time of paving
    B. make a survey of the existing pavement elevations and a survey of the final pavement elevations and check that the thickness requirements are met
    C. check that the amount of asphalt delivered is adequate to meet the depth requirements of the area to be paved
    D. take core borings to determine if the thickness meets specifications

16. The maximum roller speed for steel tired rollers paving asphalt concrete is a maximum of _____ mile(s) per hour.

    A. 7   B. 5   C. 3   D. 1

17. The weathered or dry surface appearing on a relatively new pavement can generally be attributed to

    A. inadequate rolling
    B. oversized coarse aggregate in the mix
    C. excessive amount of fine aggregate
    D. insufficient asphalt in the mix

18. Construction contracts for highways have items paid either by unit price or lump sum. The one of the following that is usually a lump sum item on a highway contract is

    A. excavation   B. paving
    C. fencing   D. demolition

19. Highway roadway subgrades are usually required to have a relative density of _____ percent.

    A. 80 to 84   B. 85 to 89   C. 90 to 95   D. 100

20. A *profile* of a highway is

    A. the section taken along the centerline of the highway
    B. an aesthetic landscape sketch of the highway
    C. used to determine the line of the highway
    D. used to locate overpasses

21. A culvert as used under a highway is usually installed

    A. as a relief sewer
    B. as a bypass for a stream
    C. in a stream bed
    D. to carry sanitary and storm flow

22. A mass diagram as related to highway construction work is used to

    A. minimize traffic congestion
    B. compute payment for hauling excavation and fill
    C. find the largest feasible radius of curvature for a horizontal curve
    D. help determine the depth of an asphalt concrete pavement

23. The geometric shape of a vertical curve on a highway is a(n)

    A. parabola   B. hyperbola   C. circle   D. ellipse

24. When cast iron bell and spigot pipe is used in sewer construction, the joint is usually sealed with

    A. lead   B. tin
    C. cement mortar   D. oakum

25. A planimeter is used to measure

    A. location   B. area   C. elevation   D. angles

KEY (CORRECT ANSWERS)

1. C
2. D
3. B
4. B
5. C

6. D
7. C
8. B
9. B
10. C

11. D
12. D
13. A
14. B
15. A

16. C
17. D
18. D
19. C
20. A

21. C
22. B
23. A
24. A
25. B

TEST 2

DIRECTIONS: Each question or incomplete statement is followed by several suggested answers or completions. Select the one that BEST answers the question or completes the statement. *PRINT THE LETTER OF THE CORRECT ANSWER IN THE SPACE AT THE RIGHT.*

1. A witness stake is usually used in surveying primarily as 1._____

    A. proof that a given location has been surveyed
    B. an aid in locating a surveying stake
    C. a marker to prevent a stake being disturbed
    D. an offset stake

2. Before the contractor begins work on a sewer or highway project, a detailed survey is made of all existing structures that may be affected by the construction in order to 2._____

    A. protect against false claims for damage
    B. insure that the contractor causes no damage to property
    C. insure that existing elevations conform to elevations on the contract drawings
    D. uncover potential weaknesses in structures

3. The optimum moisture content of a given soil will result in the 3._____

    A. plastic limit of the soil is reached
    B. liquid limit of the soil is reached
    C. porosity of the soil is at its maximum
    D. soil is compacted to its maximum dry density

4. The letters SC for soil means 4._____

    A. silty clay   B. clayey sand
    C. sandy clay   D. clayey silt

5. A cradle is used under a large precast circular concrete pipe sewer. The purpose of the cradle is mainly to 5._____

    A. minimize the settlement of the earth on the sides of the sewer
    B. minimize the settlement under the pipe
    C. strengthen the pipe against collapse
    D. resist side pressure against the pipe

6. The joints on laid precast concrete pipe were poorly made.
The consequence of this poor workmanship is most likely 6._____

    A. the pipe will settle
    B. the pipe may collapse
    C. the water table may be adversely affected
    D. there will be excessive infiltration

7. An existing sewer is to connect into a new deep manhole for a new sewer. According to old plans for the existing sewer, the elevation of the existing sewer is 1/2 inch lower than shown on the plan.
Of the following, the BEST action that the inspector can take is 7._____

43

A. call his superior for instructions
B. do nothing
C. have the contractor relay the existing pipe to the theoretical elevation shown on the old plan
D. have an adjustable connection placed between the old pipe and the new manhole

8. The contractor proposes using a cement-lime mix for cement mortar to be used in building a manhole.
   This is

   A. *good* practice as this is a more workable mortar
   B. *good* practice as the mortar is slow setting
   C. *poor* practice because the mortar weakens in a wet environment
   D. *poor* practice as a cement-lime mortar is more porous than a cement mortar

   8.___

9. Most serious claims for extra payment on large sewer contracts result from

   A. soil conditions that are markedly different from those that were presented by the owner
   B. the inspectors being unreasonable in their demands
   C. delay in making the areas available for work
   D. the fact that the method of construction required by the owner proved to be unworkable

   9.___

10. Unconsolidated fill is at pipe laying depth. Of the following, the BEST action that an inspector can take is to

    A. have the unconsolidated fill removed and replaced with concrete
    B. have the unconsolidated fill removed and replaced with sound fill
    C. report this matter to your supervisor for his consideration
    D. ask the contractor to consolidate the fill

    10.___

11. Buried debris not shown on the borings is uncovered near the surface of an excavation for a deep sewer. Of the following, the BEST action for an inspector to take is to

    A. record the depth and extent of the debris in the event of a claim
    B. do nothing as this has no effect on the final product
    C. notify the contractor that there is no valid claim for the extra work required
    D. be certain that the debris is not used in the backfill

    11.___

12. A come-along or deadman is sometimes used in the laying of large precast concrete pipe to insure

    A. the pipe is at proper grade
    B. the pipe is on proper line
    C. that the pipe will not subsequently settle
    D. that the pipe is properly seated

    12.___

13. In laying sewers,

    A. accuracy in the line of the sewer is more important than accuracy in the grade of the sewer
    B. accuracy in the grade of the sewer is more important than accuracy in the line of the sewer

    13.___

C. accuracy in the line and grade of the sewer are equally important
D. since the sewer is underground, accuracy is not required either for line or grade

14. A sewer contract is given out with a price per foot of sewer for different diameter sewers. After the contract is let, the low bidder is required to give a breakdown of his price per foot of sewer to include excavation, sewer in place, backfill, and restoration. The purpose of this breakdown is to

    A. facilitate partial payments
    B. insure the bid is not unbalanced
    C. enable the agency to gather up-to-date cost data for future projects
    D. make it easier to price extra work

15. The house sewer runs from the house to the main line sewer. The size of this sewer is most frequently _____ inches.

    A. 4   B. 5   C. 6   D. 8

16. A line on centerline at the inside bottom of a pipe or conduit is known as the

    A. convert   B. invert   C. subvert   D. exvert

17. One of the most important elements of excavating for sewer construction is to maintain the specified width of the trench at the top of the pipe. If the width at the top of the pipe is too great,

    A. this may cause excessive settlement of the pipe
    B. this may cause excessive settlement of the backfill damaging the final pavement
    C. this may place excessive load on the pipe
    D. it may undermine utilities adjacent to the pipe

18. Wellpoints are used in sewer construction mainly to

    A. keep water out of the trench due to a heavy rainstorm
    B. keep water out of the excavation and subsoil to avoid excessive pressure on the sheeting
    C. prevent a boil from forming in the trench
    D. lower the water table to facilitate construction of the sewer

19. When a trench excavation uses soldier beams and horizontal sheeting for support, the minimum number of braces for each soldier beam is

    A. 1   B. 2   C. 3   D. 4

20. Bell and spigot pipe should be laid _____ with the bell end pointed _____.

    A. downstream; upstream
    B. downstream; downstream
    C. upstream; upstream
    D. upstream; downstream

21. The specifications state that house sewers should be laid at a grade of not less than 2%. In 40 feet of house sewer, the change in grade for 40 feet should be most nearly _____ inches.

    A. 8   B. 8 1/2   C. 9   D. 9 1/2

4 (#2)

22. Two percent grade on a house sewer is equal to most nearly _____ inch per foot. 22._____

   A. 1/8 B. 3/16 C. 1/4 D. 5/16

23. When working underground in spaces that are closed and confined, such as manholes, the gas that is dangerous and most likely of the following to be present is 23._____

   A. carbon monoxide B. carbon dioxide
   C. ammonia D. methane

24. Of the following, air entrained cement would most likely be used in 24._____

   A. concrete roadways
   B. precast concrete pipe
   C. precast concrete manholes
   D. the cradle for precast concrete pipe

25. A slump cone is filled to overflowing in _____ layer(s). 25._____

   A. one B. two separate
   C. three separate D. four separate

KEY (CORRECT ANSWERS)

1. B   11. A
2. A   12. D
3. D   13. B
4. B   14. A
5. B   15. C

6. D   16. B
7. B   17. C
8. C   18. D
9. A   19. B
10. C 20. C

21. D
22. C
23. D
24. A
25. C

EXAMINATION SECTION
TEST 1

DIRECTIONS: Each question or incomplete statement is followed by several suggested answers or completions. Select the one that BEST answers the question or completes the statement. *PRINT THE LETTER OF THE CORRECT ANSWER IN THE SPACE AT THE RIGHT.*

1. A sheet asphalt pavement is to have a compacted thickness of 1 1/2 inches. The length of the teeth on an asphalt rake to be used for this pavement should be at least _____ inches.

    A. 1 1/2   B. 2   C. 2 1/2   D. 3

2. The LARGEST particles in the surface course of a sheet asphalt pavement consist of

    A. sand
    B. broken rock
    C. rock dust or powder
    D. small pebbles

3. A scarifier would be used to

    A. clean around manhole castings
    B. break up old asphalt surfaces
    C. repair wooden handles on tools
    D. spread asphaltic cement

4. Which of the following procedures is BEST when dumping the mixture for the base course of a sheet asphalt pavement? (The mixture is to be finally spread by hand.) Have the truck

    A. move as it is emptied to spread the mixture over the area where it will be placed
    B. dump the mixture in one spot in the middle of the area where it will be placed
    C. dump in small piles over the area to be covered
    D. dump outside the area to be paved

5. On sheet asphalt pavement, a surface heater would MOST likely be used to heat the

    A. base course before placing the surface course
    B. surface course so that it can be removed without destroying the base course
    C. surface course before rolling it
    D. concrete base before placing the binder course on it

6. A thin fuel oil is sometimes sprayed on the inner surface of the body of an asphalt truck. This is done to

    A. prevent the mixture from sticking to the truck
    B. keep the mixture hot during the trip from the plant to the job
    C. lubricate the mixture
    D. make the mixture more workable

7. When backfilling a deep hole before placing an asphalt patch, it is BEST to backfill

    A. the entire hole before compacting
    B. in small layers, compacting each layer evenly
    C. in small layers, compacting each layer only near the sides of the hole
    D. the entire hole and then wet down the fill before compacting

8. You are raking out a sheet asphalt mixture and you find that the mixture is full of lumps. You know that

   A. this is not unusual
   B. the mixture is too hot
   C. you should break up the lumps
   D. the mixture should not be used

9. New brick pavement would MOST likely be found on

   A. tunnel roadways   B. residential streets
   C. business streets   D. parkways

10. When filling cracks in an asphaltic pavement, it is BEST to keep the filler

    A. slightly below the surface of the pavement to permit expansion and extraction
    B. even with the surface of the pavement so that there are no bumps
    C. slightly above the surfaces of the pavement so that traffic can wear the patch smooth
    D. considerably above the surface of the pavement because the filler is much softer than the pavement

11. Of the following materials, those MOST likely to be used for curbs are

    A. steel and granite   B. cast iron and granite
    C. marble and bluestone   D. cast iron and concrete

12. Of the following fuels, the one that would MOST likely be used in a fire wagon for heating tools is

    A. charcoal   B. gasoline
    C. oil   D. compressed gas

13. Before applying the asphalt surface, the binder course should be

    A. clean and dry
    B. clean and damp
    C. dry and sprinkled with sand
    D. damp and sprinkled with sand

14. Concrete is a mixture of cement and

    A. water and sand
    B. sand and broken stone
    C. broken stone and water
    D. sand, water, and broken stone

15. The roller should continue to roll the surface course of a sheet asphalt pavement until

    A. all roller marks are eliminated and the mixture is well compressed
    B. the mixture has cooled to air temperature
    C. the end of the working day
    D. the next section is placed and ready for rolling

16. If the mixture sticks to the rolls of the roller, the BEST thing to do is to 16._____

    A. spray water over the rolls with a hose
    B. pour buckets of water over the rolls
    C. mop the rolls with water
    D. wait until the mixture cools

17. A template is used 17._____

    A. as a surface upon which a hot asphaltic mix is dumped
    B. to determine temperature in a tool heater
    C. to break up asphalt paving
    D. as a guide in shaping the surface of a pavement

18. A paving crew can place and finish 1,000 square yards of binder course in one day or it can place and finish 500 square yards of surface course in one day. 18._____
    To pave a street one mile long, the BEST way for the crew to work is

    A. place and finish all the binder course before starting the surface course
    B. never place more binder course than can be covered with a finished surface course the same day
    C. place and finish binder course one day and spend the next two days placing and finishing surface course
    D. place the binder course over one-half the width of the street for the length of two blocks, then place the surface course and finish it

19. The BEST way to lift a heavy object is to 19._____

    A. keep legs widespread and stiff, bending over to grasp object
    B. place feet about shoulder width apart and bend at the knees to reach down to the object
    C. keep legs stiff and close together, bending forward to reach the object
    D. get a good footing, keep your back straight, and lift quickly

20. The head of a cutting bar used to cut asphalt pavement has mushroomed under the blows of the sledge hammer. This cutting bar should be 20._____

    A. continued in use as mushrooming is normal and cannot be prevented
    B. thrown away as it is dangerous
    C. returned to the shop for re-dressing and then used again
    D. heated red hot and plunged into cold water

21. Which of the following articles is LEAST likely to qualify as protective clothing for an asphalt worker? 21._____

    A. Hard hat
    B. Shoes with reinforced toes
    C. Heavy denim pants
    D. Heavy canvas gloves

22. While using a pick, you discover that the handle is loose. The BEST thing to do is to
    A. finish the job as is and then repair the pick
    B. tape the head to the handle and finish the job
    C. hold the head with one hand and the handle with the other and finish the job
    D. stop work and get a new pick or repair this one

23. The proper width of a lute for sheet asphalt work is about _____ feet.
    A. 2 B. 4 C. 6 D. 8

24. Smoothing irons would LEAST likely be used
    A. to iron in asphaltic cement adjacent to curbs
    B. to smooth defects in the surface of the finished surface in the center of the road
    C. at joints
    D. at contact surfaces

25. The speed of a roller working sheet asphalt should not exceed, in miles per hour,
    A. 1/2 B. 3 C. 9 D. 18

KEY (CORRECT ANSWERS)

1. D   11. A
2. A   12. C
3. B   13. A
4. D   14. D
5. B   15. A

6. A   16. C
7. B   17. D
8. D   18. B
9. A   19. B
10. B 20. C

21. A
22. D
23. C
24. B
25. B

TEST 2

DIRECTIONS: Each question or incomplete statement is followed by several suggested answers or completions. Select the one that BEST answers the question or completes the statement. *PRINT THE LETTER OF THE CORRECT ANSWER IN THE SPACE AT THE RIGHT.*

1. Surfaces which should be painted with hot asphaltic cement before the surface mixture is laid include

    A. manhole covers
    B. tops of curbs
    C. edges of headers
    D. surface on which mixture is placed

    1.____

2. After a sheet asphalt pavement has been laid, it is sometimes sprinkled with

    A. water   B. salt   C. kerosene   D. cement

    2.____

3. While a sheet asphalt paving job is in progress, there is a sudden rain storm. The work should be

    A. stopped immediately
    B. continued until the mixture on the job is laid and finished
    C. continued until the mixture on the job and in transit is laid and finished
    D. continued until a good stopping place is reached

    3.____

4. Asphaltic concrete differs from sheet asphalt mix. The difference which is MOST readily apparent is due to the fact that asphaltic concrete

    A. contains more asphaltic cement
    B. contains broken stone
    C. is made with a softer asphaltic cement
    D. is lighter in cold

    4.____

5. A curb is usually associated with

    A. a driveway crossing a sidewalk
    B. the sidewall of a tire
    C. a catch basin installation
    D. surveyors' marks

    5.____

6. A 1:2:3 1/4 mix would MOST likely refer to

    A. concrete   B. sheet asphalt mix
    C. asphaltic concrete   D. plaster

    6.____

7. Adding gasoline to asphaltic cement would make the asphalt

    A. softer   B. harder
    C. darker in color   D. useless

    7.____

8. Emulsified asphalt would be used for

    A. sheet asphalt wearing course
    B. sheet asphalt binder course
    C. asphaltic concrete
    D. cold patch mix

    8.____

9. A specification reads: Anchors provided for securing the curb in position shall be such shape and size, and attached in such manner and at such points as designated on the plans.
   This specification applies to _____ curbs.

   A. granite   B. bluestone   C. concrete   D. steel

10. The outside of a curve in a highway should be built higher than the inside. The reason for this is to

    A. drain water better
    B. strengthen the most used part of the pavement
    C. prevent cars skidding on the pavement
    D. prevent ice from forming on the pavement

11. When concrete is mixed by hand, the BEST method is to first mix together

    A. sand and cement   B. cement and water
    C. sand and broken rock   D. broken rock and cement

12. Some asphaltic cement is accidentally spilled on the surface of a sheet asphalt surface course during rolling.
    This is

    A. *good*, because it makes a more waterproof surface
    B. *good*, because it strengthens the course
    C. *bad*, because the asphaltic cement is expensive
    D. *bad*, because the asphaltic cement will stick to the rolls of the roller

13. Before a seal coat is rolled, it should be

    A. spread with broken stones
    B. allowed to cool
    C. heated with a surface heater
    D. raked out

14. The EASIEST way to determine whether a bituminous material is an asphalt or a tar is to use your sense of

    A. sight   B. smell   C. taste   D. touch

15. The markings on a drum of cut-back asphalt cannot be read. To determine whether it is slow-, medium-, or rapid-curing, you heat a sample. The odor it gives off is like hot motor oil. The material is _____ -curing.

    A. rapid   B. medium
    C. slow   D. either rapid- or slow

16. Sheet asphalt laid yesterday was rolled to a feather edge. Before today's mixture is placed against the cold edge, the edge should be

    A. heated   B. cut back and painted
    C. painted   D. smoothed

17. A round hole about 9 inches across has developed in the surface course of a sheet asphalt pavement. The exposed surface of the binder course shows it to be in good condition. The hole should be filled with

    A. high early strength concrete
    B. a mixture similar to the surface course mix
    C. a mixture similar to the base course mix
    D. asphaltic cement

17.____

18. A square cut 3'0" x 3'0" has been made in a sheet asphalt pavement for a water connection. The sides of the cut are vertical and continuous through surface binder, and concrete base course. Before starting repairs, the foreman directed that a strip of asphalt 6" wide be removed all around the opening, making the opening in the asphalt a perfect square, 4'0" on a side.
    Removing this asphalt was

    A. *wrong,* because it increased the size of the asphalt patch by more than 75%
    B. *right,* because it allowed a more effective patch to be placed
    C. *wrong;* the edge of the asphalt opening should be irregular
    D. *right,* because the enlarged opening requires very little extra work on the part of the asphalt gang

18.____

19. Several cracks varying in width from 1/16 to 1/8 inch have appeared in an asphalt pavement. The BEST thing to do is

    A. nothing
    B. fill the cracks with asphaltic cement
    C. fill the cracks with sand, then pour in asphaltic cement
    D. fill the cracks with sand which has been coated lightly with asphaltic cement

19.____

20. A fat spot has developed on an asphalt macadam pavement. The BEST way to repair this spot is to

    A. add sand to the surface
    B. add broken stone to the surface
    C. heat it and cut away the excess asphalt
    D. shave the spot with a bulldozer

20.____

21. Cracks varying in width from 1/4 to 3/4 inch have developed in a concrete pavement. The FIRST step in repairing the pavement is to fill the cracks with

    A. a mixture of cement and water
    B. a mixture of sand, cement, and water
    C. asphaltic cement
    D. sand which has been coated lightly with asphaltic cement

21.____

22. The danger of fire would be greatest when working with

    A. rapid-curing cut-back asphalt
    B. medium-curing cut-back asphalt
    C. slow-curing cut-back asphalt
    D. asphaltic cement

22.____

23. Asphaltic cement is usually shipped in

   A. sacks   B. kegs   C. barrels   D. drums

24. The following statement applies to the construction of concrete curbs: In depositing, the concrete shall be tamped and the aggregate shall be carefully spaded away from the front forms.
    The spading is done to

   A. give a slope to the face of the curb
   B. make the face of the curb smooth
   C. make a honeycombed concrete
   D. remove the excess water

25. A colorless membrane is sometimes sprayed over a freshly laid concrete. The purpose of this is to

   A. prevent children from marring the surface
   B. provide additional strength while the concrete is wet
   C. make the concrete surface very smooth
   D. prevent evaporation of the water in the concrete

KEY (CORRECT ANSWERS)

1. C	11. A
2. D	12. D
3. C	13. A
4. B	14. B
5. A	15. C
6. A	16. B
7. A	17. B
8. D	18. B
9. D	19. A
10. C	20. C

21. D
22. A
23. D
24. B
25. D

WORK SCHEDULING

EXAMINATION SECTION
TEST 1

DIRECTIONS: Each question or incomplete statement is followed by several suggested answers or completions. Select the one that BEST answers the question or completes the statement. *PRINT THE LETTER OF THE CORRECT ANSWER IN THE SPACE AT THE RIGHT.*

Questions 1-6.

DIRECTIONS: Questions 1 through 6 are to be answered SOLELY on the basis of the information given in the ELEVATOR OPERATORS' WORK SCHEDULE shown below.

ELEVATOR OPERATORS' WORK SCHEDULE				
Operator	Hours of Work	A.M. Relief Period	Lunch Hour	P.M. Relief Period
Anderson	8:30-4:30	10:20-10:30	12:00-1:00	2:20-2:30
Carter	8:00-4:00	10:10-10:20	11:45-12:45	2:30-2:40
Daniels	9:00-5:00	10:20-10:30	12:30-1:30	3:15-3:25
Grand	9:30-5:30	11:30-11:40	1:00-2:00	4:05-4:15
Jones	7:45-3:45	9:45-9:55	11:30-12:30	2:05-2:15
Lewis	9:45-5:45	11:40-11:50	1:15-2:15	4:20-4:30
Nance	8:45-4:45	10:50-11:00	12:30-1:30	3:05-3:15
Perkins	8:00-4:00	10:00-10:10	12:00-1:00	2:40-2:50
Russo	7:45-3:45	9:30-9:40	11:30-12:30	2:10-2:20
Smith	9:45-5:45	11:45-11:55	1:15-2:15	4:05-4:15

1. The two operators who are on P.M. relief at the SAME time are

   A. Anderson and Daniels B. Carter and Perkins
   C. Jones and Russo   D. Grand and Smith

2. Of the following, the two operators who have the SAME lunch hour are

   A. Anderson and Perkins B. Daniels and Russo
   C. Grand and Smith   D. Nance and Russo

3. At 12:15, the number of operators on their lunch hour is

   A. 3   B. 4   C. 5   D. 6

4. The operator who has an A.M. relief period right after Perkins and a P.M. relief period right before Perkins is

   A. Russo   B. Nance   C. Daniels   D. Carter

5. The number of operators who are scheduled to be working at 4:40 is

   A. 5   B. 6   C. 7   D. 8

6. According to the schedule, it is MOST correct to say that

    A. no operator has a relief period during the time that another operator has a lunch hour
    B. each operator has to wait an identical amount of time between the end of lunch and the beginning of P.M. relief period
    C. no operator has a relief period before 9:45 or after 4:00
    D. each operator is allowed a total of 1 hour and 20 minutes for lunch hour and relief periods

KEY (CORRECT ANSWERS)

1. D
2. A
3. C
4. D
5. A
6. D

TEST 2

DIRECTIONS: Each question or incomplete statement is followed by several suggested answers or completions. Select the one that BEST answers the question or completes the statement. *PRINT THE LETTER OF THE CORRECT ANSWER IN THE SPACE AT THE RIGHT.*

Questions 1-7.

DIRECTIONS: Questions 1 through 7 are to be answered SOLELY on the basis of the time sheet and instructions given below.

The following time sheet indicates the times that seven laundry workers arrived and left each day for the week of August 23. The times they arrived for work are shown under the heading IN, and the times they left are shown under the heading OUT. The letter (P) indicates time which was used for personal business. Time used for this purpose is charged to annual leave. Lunch time is one-half hour from noon to 12:30 P.M. and is not accounted for on this time record.

The employees on this shift are scheduled to work from 8:00 A.M. to 4:00 P.M. Lateness is charged to annual leave. Reporting after 8:00 A.M. is considered late.

	MON.		TUES.		WED.		THURS.		FRI.	
	AM IN	PM OUT	AM IN	PM OUT	AM IN	PM OUT	AM IN	PM OUT	AM IN	PM OUT
Baxter	7:50	4:01	7:49	4:07	8:00	4:07	8:20	4:00	7:42	4:03
Gardner	8:02	4:00	8:20	4:00	8:05	3:30(P)	8:00	4:03	8:00	4:07
Clements	8:00	4:04	8:03	4:01	7:59	4:00	7:54	4:06	7:59	4:00
Tompkins	7:56	4:00	Annual leave		8:00	4:07	7:59	4:00	8:00	4:01
Wagner	8:04	4:03	7:40	4:00	7:53	4:04	8:00	4:09	7:53	4:00
Patterson	8:00	2:30(P)	8:15	4:04	Sick leave		7:45	4:00	7:59	4:04
Cunningham	7:43	4:02	7:50	4:00	7:59	4:02	8:00	4:10	8:00	4:00

1. Which one of the following laundry workers did NOT have any time charged to annual leave or sick leave during the week?

   A. Gardner   B. Clements   C. Tompkins   D. Cunningham

   1.____

2. On which day did ALL the laundry workers arrive on time?

   A. Monday   B. Wednesday   C. Thursday   D. Friday

   2.____

3. Which of the following laundry workers used time to take care of personal business?

   A. Baxter and Clements   B. Patterson and Cunningham
   C. Gardner and Patterson   D. Wagner and Tompkins

   3.____

4. How many laundry workers were late on Monday?

   A. 1   B. 2   C. 3   D. 4

   4.____

5. Which one of the following laundry workers arrived late on three of the five days?

   A. Baxter   B. Gardner   C. Wagner   D. Patterson

   5.____

57

6. The percentage of laundry workers reporting to work late on Tuesday is MOST NEARLY   6._____
   A. 15%   B. 25%   C. 45%   D. 50%

7. The percentage of laundry workers that were absent for an entire day during the week is MOST NEARLY   7._____
   A. 6%   B. 9%   C. 15%   D. 30%

KEY (CORRECT ANSWERS)

1. D
2. D
3. C
4. B
5. B
6. C
7. D

TEST 3

Questions 1-9.

DIRECTIONS: Questions 1 through 9 are to be answered SOLELY on the basis of the following information and timesheet given below.

The following is a foreman's timesheet for his crew for one week. The hours worked each day or the reason the man was off on that day are shown on the sheet. *R* means rest day. *A* means annual leave. *S* means sick leave. Where a man worked only part of a day, both the number of hours worked and the number of hours taken off are entered. The reason for absence is entered in parentheses next to the number of hours taken off.

Name	Saturday	Sunday	Monday	Tuesday	Wednesday	Thursday	Friday
Smith	R	R	7	7	7	3 4(A)	7
Jones	R	7	7	7	7	7	R
Green	R	R	7	7	S	S	S
White	R	R	7	7	A	7	7
Doe	7	7	7	7	7	R	R
Brown	R	R	A	7	7	7	7
Black	R	R	S	7	7	7	7
Reed	R	R	7	7	7	7	S
Roe	R	R	A	7	7	7	7
Lane	7	R	R	7	7	A	S

1. The caretaker who worked EXACTLY 21 hours during the week is

    A. Lane   B. Roe   C. Smith   D. White

2. The TOTAL number of hours worked by all caretakers during the week is

    A. 268   B. 276   C. 280   D. 288

3. The two days of the week on which MOST caretakers were off are

    A. Thursday and Friday
    B. Friday and Saturday
    C. Saturday and Sunday
    D. Sunday and Monday

4. The day on which three caretakers were off on sick leave is

    A. Monday   B. Friday   C. Saturday   D. Sunday

5. The two workers who took LEAST time off during the week are

    A. Doe and Reed
    B. Jones and Doe
    C. Reed and Smith
    D. Smith and Jones

6. The caretaker who worked the LEAST number of hours during the week is

    A. Brown   B. Green   C. Lane   D. Roe

7. The caretakers who did NOT work on Thursday are

    A. Doe, White, and Smith
    B. Green, Doe, and Lane
    C. Green, Doe, and Smith
    D. Green, Lane, and Smith

59

8. The day on which one caretaker worked ONLY 3 hours is 8.____
   A. Friday   B. Saturday   C. Thursday   D. Wednesday

9. The day on which ALL caretakers worked is 9.____
   A. Monday   B. Thursday   C. Tuesday   D. Wednesday

KEY (CORRECT ANSWERS)

1. A
2. B
3. C
4. B
5. B

6. B
7. B
8. C
9. C

TEST 4

Questions 1-6.

DIRECTIONS: Questions 1 through 6 are to be answered SOLELY on the basis of the table below which shows the initial requests made by staff for vacation. It is to be used with the RULES AND GUIDELINES to make the decisions and judgments called for in each of the questions.

VACATION REQUESTS FOR THE ONE YEAR PERIOD FROM MAY 1, YEAR X THROUGH APRIL 30, YEAR Y				
Name	Work Assignment	Date Appointed	Accumulated Annual Leave Days	Vacation Periods Requested
DeMarco	MVO	Mar. 2003	25	May 3-21; Oct. 25-Nov. 5
Moore	Dispatcher	Dec. 1997	32	May 24-June 4; July 12-16
Kingston	MVO	Apr. 2007	28	May 24-June 11; Feb. 7-25
Green	MVO	June 2006	26	June 7-18; Sept. 6-24
Robinson	MVO	July 2008	30	June 28-July 9; Nov. 15-26
Reilly	MVO	Oct. 2009	23	July 5-9; Jan. 31-Mar. 3
Stevens	MVO	Sept. 1996	31	July 5-23; Oct. 4-29
Costello	MVO	Sept. 1998	31	July 5-30; Oct. 4-22
Maloney	Dispatcher	Aug. 1992	35	July 5-Aug. 6; Nov. 1-5
Hughes	Director	Feb. 1990	38	July 26-Sept. 3
Lord	MVO	Jan. 2010	20	Aug. 9-27; Feb. 7-25
Diaz	MVO	Dec. 2009	28	Aug. 9-Sept. 10
Krimsky	MVO	May 2006	22	Oct. 18-22: Nov. 22-Dec. 10

RULES AND GUIDELINES

1. The two Dispatchers cannot be on vacation at the same time, nor can a Dispatcher be on vacation at the same time as the Director.

2. For the period June 1 through September 30, not more than three MVO's can be on vacation at the same time.

3. For the period October 1 through May 31, not more than two MVO's at a time can be on vacation.

4. In cases where the same vacation time is requested by too many employees for all of them to be given the time under the rules, the requests of those who have worked the longest will be granted.

5. No employee may take more leave days than the number of annual leave days accumulated and shown in the table.

6. All vacation periods shown in the table and described in the questions below begin on a Monday and end on a Friday.

7. Employees work a five-day week (Monday through Friday). They are off weekends and holidays with no charges to leave balances. When a holiday falls on a Saturday or Sunday, employees are given the following Monday off without charge to annual leave.

2 (#4)

8. Holidays:
   May 31   October 25   January 1
   July 4   November 2   February 12
   September 6 November 25   February 21
   October 11   December 25   February 21

9. An employee shall be given any part of his initial requests that is permissible under the above rules and shall have first right to it despite any further adjustment of schedule.

---

1. Until adjustments in the vacation schedule can be made, the vacation dates that can be approved for Krimsky are

   A. Oct. 18-22; Nov. 22-Dec. 10
   B. Oct. 18-22; Nov. 29-Dec. 10
   C. Oct. 18-22 *only*
   D. Nov. 22-Dec. 10 *only*

2. Until adjustments in the vacation schedule can be made, the vacation dates that can be approved for Maloney are

   A. July 5-Aug. 6; Nov. 1-5
   B. July 5-23; Nov. 1-5
   C. July 5-9; Nov. 1-5
   D. Nov. 1-5 *only*

3. According to the table, Lord wants a vacation in August and another in February. Until adjustments in the vacation schedule can be made, he can be allowed to take _____ of the August vacation and _____ of the February vacation.

   A. all; none
   B. all; almost half
   C. almost all; almost half
   D. almost half; all

4. Costello cannot be given all the vacation he has requested because

   A. the MVO's who have more seniority than he has have requested time he wishes
   B. he does not have enough accumulated annual leave
   C. a dispatcher is applying for vacation at the same time as Costello
   D. there are five people who want vacation in July

5. According to the table, how many leave days will DeMarco be charged for his vacation from October 25 through November 5?

   A. 10   B. 9   C. 8   D. 7

6. How many leave days will Moore use if he uses the requested vacation allowable to him under the rules?

   A. 9   B. 10   C. 14   D. 15

KEY (CORRECT ANSWERS)

1. D
2. B
3. A
4. B
5. C
6. A

TEST 5

Questions 1-8.

DIRECTIONS: Questions 1 through 8 are to be answered SOLELY on the basis of Charts I, II, III, and IV. Assume that you are the supervisor of Operators R, S, T, U, V, W, and X, and it is your responsibility to schedule their lunch hours.

The charts each represent a possible scheduling of lunch hours during a lunch period from 11:30 - 2:00. An operator-hour is one hour of time spent by one operator. Each box on the chart represents one half-hour. The boxes marked L represent the time when each operator is scheduled to have her lunch hour. For example, in Chart I, next to Operator R, the boxes for 11:30 - 12:00 and 12:00 -12:30 are marked L. This means that Operator R is scheduled to have her lunch hour from 11:30 to 12:30.

I

	11:30-12:00	12:00-12:30	12:30-1:00	1:00-1:30	1:30-2:00
R	L	L			
S		L	L		
T		L	L		
U			L	L	
V			L	L	
W				L	L
X				L	L

II

	11:30-12:00	12:00-12:30	12:30-1:00	1:00-1:30	1:30-2:00
R				L	L
S		L	L		
T	L	L			
U		L	L		
V				L	L
W				L	L
X	L	L			

III

	11:30-12:00	12:00-12:30	12:30-1:00	1:00-1:30	1:30-2:00
R	L	L			
S				L	L
T	L	L			
U			L	L	
V	L	L			
W				L	L
X				L	L

IV

	11:30-12:00	12:00-12:30	12:30-1:00	1:00-1:30	1:30-2:00
R	L	L			
S	L	L			
T		L	L		
U			L	L	
V				L	L
W				L	L
X				L	L

1. If, under the schedule represented in Chart II, Operator R has her lunch hour changed to 12:30-1:30, that leaves how many operator-hours of phone coverage from 1:00-2:00?

   A. 2   B. 2 1/2   C. 3   D. 4 1/2

2. If Operator S asks you whether she and Operator T may have the same lunch hour, you could accommodate her by using the schedule in Chart

   A. I   B. II   C. III   D. IV

3. From past experience you know that the part of the lunch period when the phones are busiest is from 12:30-1:30. Which chart shows the BEST phone coverage from 12:30 to 1:30?

   A. I   B. II   C. III   D. IV

4. At least three operators have the same lunch hour according to Chart(s)

   A. II and III   B. II and IV
   C. III only   D. IV only

5. Which chart would provide the POOREST phone coverage during the period 12:00-1:30, based on total number of operator-hours from 12:00 to 1:30?

    A. I   B. II   C. III   D. IV

5.____

6. Which chart would make it possible for U, W, and X to have the same lunch hour?

    A. I   B. II   C. III   D. IV

6.____

7. The portion of the lunch period during which the telephones are least busy is 11:30-12:30.
Which chart is MOST likely to have been designed with that fact in mind?

    A. I   B. II   C. III   D. IV

7.____

8. Assume that you have decided to use Chart IV to schedule your operators' lunch hours on a specific day. Operator T asks you if she can have her lunch hour changed to 1:00-2:00.
If you grant her request, how many operators will be working during the period 12:00 to 12:30?

    A. 1   B. 2   C. 4   D. 5

8.____

KEY (CORRECT ANSWERS)

1. D
2. A
3. B
4. A
5. A
6. C
7. C
8. D

TEST 6

Questions 1-13.

DIRECTIONS: Questions 1 through 13 consist of a statement. You are to indicate whether the statement is TRUE (T) or FALSE (F). *PRINT THE LETTER OF THE CORRECT ANSWER IN THE SPACE AT THE RIGHT.* Questions 1 through 13 are to be answered SOLELY on the basis of the information given in the table below.

DEPARTMENT OF FERRIES ATTENDANTS WORK ASSIGNMENT - JULY 2003				
Name	Year Employed	Ferry Assigned	Hours of Work	Lunch Period	Days Off
Adams	1999	Hudson	7 AM - 3 PM	11-12	Fri. and Sat.
Baker	1992	Monroe	7 AM - 3 PM	11-12	Sun. and Mon.
Gunn	1995	Troy	8 AM - 4 PM	12-1	Fri. and Sat.
Hahn	1989	Erie	9 AM - 5 PM	1-2	Sat. and Sun.
King	1998	Albany	7 AM - 3 PM	11-12	Sun. and Mon.
Nash	1993	Hudson	11 AM - 7 PM	3-4	Sun. and Mon.
Olive	2003	Fulton	10 AM - 6 PM	2-3	Sat. and Sun.
Queen	2002	Albany	11 AM - 7 PM	3-4	Fri. and Sat.
Rose	1990	Troy	11 AM - 7 PM	3-4	Sun. and Mon.
Smith	1991	Monroe	10 AM - 6 PM	2-3	Fri. and Sat.

1. The chart shows that there are only five (5) ferries being used.
2. The attendant who has been working the LONGEST time is Rose.
3. The Troy has one more attendant assigned to it than the Erie.
4. Two (2) attendants are assigned to work from 10 P.M. to 6 A.M.
5. According to the chart, no more than one attendant was hired in any year.
6. The NEWEST employee is Olive.
7. There are as many attendants on the 7 to 3 shift as on the 11 to 7 shift.
8. MOST of the attendants have their lunch either between 12 and 1 or 2 and 3.
9. All the employees work four (4) hours before they go to lunch.
10. On the Hudson, Adams goes to lunch when Nash reports to work.
11. All the attendants who work on the 7 to 3 shift are off on Saturday and Sunday.
12. All the attendants have either a Saturday or Sunday as one of their days off.
13. At least two (2) attendants are assigned to each ferry.

KEY (CORRECT ANSWERS)

1. F
2. F
3. T
4. F
5. T

6. T
7. T
8. F
9. T
10. T

11. F
12. T
13. F

EXAMINATION SECTION
TEST 1

DIRECTIONS: Each question or incomplete statement is followed by several suggested answers or completions. Select the one that BEST answers the question or completes the statement. *PRINT THE LETTER OF THE CORRECT ANSWER IN THE SPACE AT THE RIGHT.*

1. Which one of the following statements pertaining to on-the-job training is *most usually* considered CORRECT?

    A. The foreman will get better results by praising a mechanic for a good job than criticizing him for a bad one.
    B. A mechanic who learns slowly will automatically retain more of what he learns than will a person who learns fast.
    C. An older mechanic learns more easily than does a younger person.
    D. It is best to learn the hardest part of a job first and then go on to the easier parts.

1.____

2. Of the following statements, the one which will be MOST effective in helping a foreman develop cooperation, interest, and enthusiasm among his men in performing their work is if he

    A. maintains close personal contact with his men
    B. makes work assignments in exactly the same way
    C. *covers up* when any of his men makes a serious error
    D. realizes that it is his men who will get the job done

2.____

3. Generally, the MAIN reason for a foreman to investigate accidents is to

    A. help prevent a recurrence of the accident
    B. help determine if replacement parts are needed
    C. provide information for a possible lawsuit
    D. prevent false compensation claims

3.____

4. Assume that you are having a discussion with one of your mechanics about his job performance. During the discussion, you make an unfavorable comment in between two complimentary comments.
For you to do this is a

    A. *good idea* because this makes it easier for the mechanic to be criticized
    B. *bad idea* because criticism should not be softened with any kind words
    C. *good idea* because more of your unfavorable comments will be remembered this way
    D. *bad idea* because a mechanic deserves to hear the straight truth

4.____

5. Of the following, at a face-to-face discussion with a mechanic about his job duties and responsibilities, it is MOST desirable to

    A. give the mechanic just enough knowledge to work until the next such discussion
    B. let the mechanic have a good understanding of how he is doing on the job
    C. deal with some of the mechanic's complaints but not all of them at one time
    D. remain aloof from the mechanic so the mechanic does not ask further questions

5.____

6. A foreman conducts periodic meetings for his own group of mechanics. The topics MOST often discussed at these group meetings would PROBABLY be

   A. efficiency reports, worker evaluations, and promotion opportunities
   B. disciplinary actions, grievances, and suspensions
   C. incentive awards, tenants' complaints, and employee suggestions
   D. work schedules, work procedures, and safety

7. Suppose your supervisor has asked you to prepare a written report on the morale problems of your work force. The one of the following observations about report writing that is MOST important for you to remember is to

   A. use the most difficult vocabulary you can
   B. make the report as long as possible
   C. use language appropriate for the people reading the report
   D. try to liven up your report so people will find it interesting

8. When a foreman writes a report, it is MOST important to prepare an outline because the outline

   A. will impress his supervisor
   B. will indicate areas to study more fully
   C. can serve as a handy summary at the end of the report
   D. will help him organize the material for his report

9. A newly assigned mechanic fails to carry out an assignment and claims that he did not understand the orders.
   Of the following, the BEST way to handle the situation is to

   A. take his word for it and see if it happens again
   B. have the incident noted in the employee's record and tell the employee afterwards
   C. give the assignment to another more experienced mechanic
   D. take formal disciplinary action against the mechanic to make sure that it does not happen again

10. Your supervisor makes a habit of bypassing you in issuing orders to your mechanics.
    Of the following courses of action, the BEST one for you to take in this situation is to

    A. tell your employees that they are to take orders only from you
    B. have your employees comply with the orders and have them report back directly to your supervisor
    C. talk to your supervisor and point out that the practice can be harmful to efficiency and morale
    D. tell your supervisor that he is not to give orders to your employees except in emergencies

11. You find that one of your better mechanics has become slipshod in making preventive maintenance inspections. Of the following, the BEST way to handle this situation is to

    A. warn him that if his work does not improve, you will have him transferred to another crew
    B. issue a general notice to all mechanics on the need of making thorough inspections
    C. tell the mechanic that he can no longer be relied on to make good inspections
    D. call in the mechanic and suggest ways in which he can improve his inspections

12. A necessary maintenance job has to be rotated among your men because it is a repetitious, boring type of job. Through an oversight, you assign this same job twice in a row to one of your men. When the man complains, you realize that you should have assigned the job to another man.

    Of the following statements, the one which is the BEST way to handle the situation is to tell the man that you

    A. will decide which assignments he will get
    B. made a mistake and that you will try to correct the situation
    C. gave him the job because you felt that he was the best man for it
    D. gave him the job because it was an emergency situation

12.____

13. Some foremen make it a practice to always find a fault in the work done by their mechanics, no matter how good a job the men do.
    For a foreman to do this is a

    A. *good idea* because it keeps the mechanics from feeling too confident
    B. *bad idea* because it is best for the foreman to point to major faults instead of minor ones
    C. *good idea* because it will encourage the mechanics to try harder
    D. *bad idea* because the mechanics will lose their feelings of achievement

13.____

14. A mechanic comes to you with a complaint which upon investigation clearly is of an imaginary nature.
    The BEST reason for giving his complaint serious attention is that, if the matter is not resolved, the mechanic

    A. will complain about it until someone listens
    B. will start taking time off from work
    C. can stir up the rest of the workers
    D. may go to the union about the matter

14.____

15. You are considering asking one of your mechanics for advice on a certain work project.
    For a foreman to ask advice from a subordinate would be MOST properly considered as a(n)

    A. way to get more production from the mechanic
    B. means of learning new work techniques from the mechanic
    C. compliment to the mechanic, as long as the foreman is sincere
    D. idea to keep the mechanic *on his toes* all the time

15.____

16. You assign a job to one of your experienced mechanics.
    You notice that he does the job in a way which is different from the way you do it.
    The BEST practice for you to follow in this case is to

    A. stop him and tell him how you want the job done
    B. let him do it his way and evaluate the results
    C. immediately take the mechanic off the job without an explanation
    D. wait until the job is done and then tell him that he should not change the existing methods

16.____

17. One of your mechanics comes to you and asks you for advice about a serious emotional problem he cannot handle. Which one of the following would be the BEST approach for you to take in handling this matter?

    A. Immediately tell him to stop worrying and that everything will work out.
    B. Advise him yourself based on your own experience.
    C. Listen attentively and tactfully suggest he seek professional help.
    D. Tell him that since it is his problem, he will have to find his own solution.

18. The one of the following which would indicate that a foreman's work attitude is WRONG is that he

    A. occasionally gets angry in front of his mechanics
    B. looks for good traits in his mechanics
    C. does not get too upset about his mechanics' mistakes
    D. always complains about his work

19. Of the following procedures, the one that would be LEAST effective in improving the job performance of subordinates is to

    A. have them evaluate their own performance so that they can determine how well they work
    B. help them set specific goals that are within their capabilities
    C. encourage them by commenting on a positive factor in their performance
    D. ask them directly about their personal affairs to determine if factors not related to the job are influencing their job performance

20. The one of the following instances in which it is BEST for a foreman to give a *spoken* order to his men is when

    A. many people are responsible for the job
    B. the job is a simple and routine one
    C. a mistake would have serious results
    D. many levels of supervision are involved

21. One of your mechanics, on his own initiative, is doing much more work than the other men. The man is well-liked, and all the other mechanics are doing an acceptable amount of work.
    Of the following, the BEST course of action for you to take in this case is to

    A. publicly praise the man as a model for the others
    B. tell the man in private that he should not do more work than the others
    C. allow the situation to continue unchanged
    D. criticize the others for failing to meet the standard set by the man

22. The one of the following instances in which it is BEST to give a *written* order to your men is when the

    A. job is a repetitive one
    B. job is a short one
    C. job involves many new details
    D. progress of the job can be easily checked

23. The MOST likely result that will occur if a foreman constantly *jumps to conclusions* is that he will 23._____

    A. lose the respect of his mechanics and superiors
    B. be correct in his conclusions half of the time
    C. inspire respect from his men
    D. gradually learn to make important decisions quickly

24. The one of the following statements on supervision that is MOST *likely* to be CORRECT is: 24._____

    A. Production is greatest when the foreman constantly criticizes his mechanics
    B. The foreman who consistently checks the work habits of his mechanics is able to correct many problems promptly
    C. The best way for a foreman to control his men is to give discipline for discipline's sake
    D. Occasional supervision of the work force is all that is necessary for your mechanics to work more efficiently

25. The one of the following that is the LEAST important reason for you to delegate work to a mechanic under your supervision is that 25._____

    A. the mechanic will have to learn to do the work
    B. it is a means of motivation
    C. your work load will be reduced
    D. it will reduce the mechanic's work responsibilities

KEY (CORRECT ANSWERS)

1. A   11. D
2. D   12. B
3. A   13. D
4. A   14. C
5. B   15. C

6. D   16. B
7. C   17. C
8. D   18. D
9. A   19. D
10. C   20. B

21. C
22. C
23. A
24. B
25. D

TEST 2

DIRECTIONS: Each question or incomplete statement is followed by several suggested answers or completions. Select the one that BEST answers the question or completes the statement. *PRINT THE LETTER OF THE CORRECT ANSWER IN THE SPACE AT THE RIGHT.*

1. The one of the following that is the LEAST important characteristic of a good foreman is   1.____

   A. a great deal of formal schooling
   B. sensitivity to the problems of others
   C. ability in working with people
   D. the ability to communicate with his men

2. Assume it is necessary to criticize a mechanic's attitude toward his work habits.   2.____
   Of the following, the BEST practice to follow would be to focus on

   A. the mechanic's character instead of his behavior
   B. comments you have heard about the man, rather than what you have observed
   C. general principles of how the mechanic should do his job instead of a specific incident
   D. sharing ideas and information with the mechanic rather than just giving advice

3. Of the following, the BEST method for a foreman to use when reprimanding a mechanic is to   3.____

   A. prepare a report reprimanding the mechanic and give it to him to avoid an argument
   B. reprimand the mechanic at a group meeting
   C. reprimand the mechanic in private, where no other mechanics are present
   D. ask your supervisor to reprimand the mechanic in your presence

4. Assume that upon assigning one of your mechanics to a certain job, he makes an unfavorable comment to you about the assignment.   4.____
   The one of the following possible approaches that would be BEST for you to take in this instance is for you to tell the man

   A. to do as he is told at all times
   B. that you will consider his opinion when you make further assignments
   C. to write down his comment and submit it to the suggestion program
   D. that he is probably right but that your supervisor is responsible for the assignment

5. One of your mechanics has just come back to work from sick leave and is working at a little less than peak efficiency. You decide not to say anything to the man because you once had the same illness yourself.   5.____
   For you to put yourself in another person's place is a

   A. *good idea* because a foreman should be sensitive to the feelings of his workers
   B. *bad idea* because a foreman should not give his men reason to think he is soft-hearted
   C. *good* idea because if the foreman does a favor for the mechanic, the mechanic will do a favor for the foreman
   D. *bad idea* because a foreman should expect uniform production from his men at all times

6. It would be POOR practice for a foreman to

    A. personally instruct a mechanic in a difficult maintenance procedure
    B. learn the relative abilities of his men by observing the quality of their work
    C. explain to his supervisor why work output decreased during a certain week
    D. complain about the quality of a mechanic's work to the man's co-workers

7. Of the following, the situation which would MOST severely test a foreman's supervisory skill would be

    A. the assignment of a regular job which must be expedited
    B. the absorption into the group under his supervision of a number of mechanics newly transferred to the shop
    C. the assignment to replace a foreman who has retired
    D. attempting to improve good housekeeping on the job

8. A mechanic repeatedly performs an important maintenance procedure incorrectly. In this situation, it would be MOST correct to conclude that the

    A. procedure is probably too difficult for the average mechanic
    B. written instructions for this job are incorrect
    C. foreman is exercising poor supervision
    D. mechanic has personal problems

9. If a foreman has a mechanic in his gang who is constantly passing the buck to his co-workers when jobs he has worked on turn out to be unsatisfactory, then it would be BEST for the foreman to

    A. complain about this man to the supervisor
    B. reassign him to work with different individuals
    C. give him work assignments which will fix responsibility on him
    D. let the co-workers who have been blamed deal with him in their own way

10. Of the following, the characteristic which will do the MOST to assure a foreman of the respect of his subordinates is the foreman's ability to

    A. maintain good relations with his supervisor
    B. plan work assignments in advance
    C. maintain rigid discipline
    D. technically assist his men in their work assignments

11. You notice that a mechanic in your gang wears rubber-soled shoes. As his foreman, you should

    A. *commend* him because these shoes insure safety from electrical shock
    B. *commend* him because these shoes produce less fatigue
    C. *disapprove* because these shoes are slippery and easily pierced
    D. *disapprove* because these shoes rot quickly when in contact with grease and oil

12. You are asked by your supervisor to have your men use a newly designed tester. Of the following, the information your supervisor would be MOST interested in obtaining from you would be

    A. an estimate of the durability of the new tester
    B. whether better production can be secured with the new tester
    C. the space requirements for the new tester
    D. the power requirements for the new tester

13. An *impartial* foreman is one who is

    A. sincere B. watchful C. industrious D. fair

14. To be MOST effective, a report should be

    A. simple and concise
    B. long and impressive
    C. written with perfect grammar and punctuation
    D. typed instead of written

15. If one of your mechanics comes to work obviously drunk, the BEST thing to do is to

    A. give the man an easy job where he can't hurt himself
    B. let the man *sleep it off* in the morning and put him to work when the effects have apparently worn off
    C. send the man home
    D. give the man a hard job where he can *sweat it out*

16. Keeping tools in good condition does NOT

    A. cut costs
    B. make work easier
    C. lessen the possibility of accidents
    D. reduce the supervision required

17. In the use of hand tools, injuries are LEAST likely to happen when working

    A. carefully
    B. with poorly conditioned and dull tools
    C. while day-dreaming
    D. with the wrong tool for the job

18. One of your mechanics offers a suggestion to improve the method of doing a job. The BEST thing to do is to tell the man that

    A. the job has always been done the same way and, therefore, it must be the best way
    B. you will check his suggestion to see whether it really is a better way of doing the job
    C. he should make the suggestion to the chief engineer
    D. he should discuss it with two other mechanics and, if they agree with him, you will try the suggested method

19. One of the mechanics in your gang complains that the other men in the gang are *riding* him.
   The FIRST action you should take is to

   A. transfer the man to another gang
   B. report the matter to your superior
   C. investigate to see if the complaint is true
   D. bring the other men in the gang up on charges

   19.____

20. One of the mechanics in your gang complains about having to do a hard job.
   The BEST thing for you to do is to

   A. ignore him
   B. explain to him that all men must do their fair share of the hard jobs
   C. tell him that his next job will be an easy one
   D. take him off this job

   20.____

21. The BEST foreman is *usually* the

   A. *best* mechanic
   B. *fastest* worker
   C. man in service the *longest*
   D. *ablest* leader

   21.____

22. Men will respect their foreman MOST if he

   A. acts sternly with them
   B. does not show favoritism
   C. is quick to criticize their errors
   D. does not enforce all the rules and regulations

   22.____

23. A newly appointed mechanic has been assigned to your gang.
   Of the following, the BEST practice to follow with this man is to

   A. immediately put him to work with the gang since his work requires no special skill
   B. allow him to do only the type of work he says he is capable of doing until he can learn the other jobs
   C. instruct the man as to how the job should be done before putting him to work
   D. give the man the most difficult job since the best method of learning is by doing

   23.____

24. Of the following, the statement that is CORRECT is:

   A. Every worker can do the same amount of work
   B. The man with the most seniority will work the fastest
   C. The strongest man will do the most work
   D. The amount of york a man does can be increased by improving morale

   24.____

25. Preventive maintenance cannot be effective unless there is (are)

   A. an efficient repair shop
   B. adequate replacement tools and equipment
   C. instructions to use care in the handling of tools and equipment
   D. regular periodic inspections of tools and equipment

   25.____

KEY (CORRECT ANSWERS)

1. A
2. D
3. C
4. B
5. A

6. D
7. B
8. C
9. C
10. B

11. C
12. B
13. D
14. A
15. C

16. D
17. A
18. B
19. C
20. B

21. D
22. B
23. C
24. D
25. D

EXAMINATION SECTION
TEST 1

DIRECTIONS: Each question or incomplete statement is followed by several suggested, answers or completions. Select the one that BEST answers the question or completes the statement. *PRINT THE LETTER OF THE CORRECT ANSWER IN THE SPACE AT THE RIGHT.*

1. Of the following, the type of water that is usually MOST suitable for mixing with normal portland cement is

   A. highly acidic water
   B. highly alkaline water
   C. water with a high sulphate content
   D. ordinary drinking water

2. Assume that the instruction manual for a machine indicates that a certain bolt must be tightened with a specified amount of force. Of the following tools, the one which should be used to tighten the bolt with the specified amount of force is a(n) _____ wrench.

   A. torque   B. adjustable
   C. stillson   D. combination

3. When a foreman delegates some of his work to a subordinate, the

   A. foreman retains final responsibility for the work
   B. foreman should not check on the work until it has been completed
   C. subordinate assumes full responsibility for the successful completion of the work
   D. subordinate is likely to lose interest and get less satisfaction from the work

4. The PRIMARY responsibility of a supervisor is to

   A. gain the confidence and make friends of all his subordinates
   B. get the work done properly
   C. satisfy his superior and gain his respect
   D. train the men in new methods for doing the work

Questions 5-10.

DIRECTIONS: Questions 5 through 10 are to be answered on the basis of the following information and Work Schedule Chart.

Assume that you are preparing a schedule of the work to be done by your crew of three laborers for one day. You have already planned some jobs as shown on the Work Schedule Chart. The work which remains to be scheduled is also listed below. The lunch hour for the three laborers is from 12:00 Noon to 1:00 P.M., and you may not plan any work during that period. Assume that the objective is to keep each of the three laborers occupied for a full day, except for their lunch hour. All laborers are qualified to perform the scheduled work. No changes are possible in the work already listed on the chart.

WORK SCHEDULE CHART
May 5

Laborer	Time 9–12	12–1	1–5
Blackburn	clean roof drain (9–11:30)		move furniture (1–5)
Gearring	clean roof drain (9–11)		
Rogers	fix ramp in front of school (9–12)		move furniture (1–5)

WORK REMAINING TO BE SCHEDULED FOR MAY 5:
Installing Shelves - requires 1 man for 2 hours
Repairing Window Blinds - requires 1 man for 1 hour
Changing Door Hardware - requires 1 man for 30 minutes
Cleaning Air Conditioner - requires 1 man for 1 hour
Pickup of Hardware at Supply Depot - requires 1 man for 1 1/2 hours

5. For which laborer and for what block of time would it be MOST appropriate to schedule the installing of shelves?

    A. Blackburn - 11:30 A.M. - 12:00 Noon
    B. Gearring - 12:30 P.M. - 1:00 P.M.
    C. Rogers - 9:00 A.M. - 10:30 A.M.
    D. Gearring - 1:00 P.M. - 3:00 P.M.

6. For which laborer and for what block of time would it be BEST to schedule the changing of door hardware?

    A. Rogers - 9:30 A.M. - 10:00 A.M.
    B. Blackburn - 11:30 A.M. - 12:00 Noon
    C. Gearring - 10:00 A.M. - 10:30 A.M.
    D. Rogers - 12:30 P.M. - 1:00 P.M.

7. For which laborer and for what block of time would it be MOST appropriate to schedule the repairing of window blinds?

    A. Rogers - 10:30 A.M. - 11:00 A.M.
    B. Gearring - 11:00 A.M. - 12:00 Noon
    C. Blackburn - 4:00 P.M. - 5:00 P.M.
    D. Gearring - 3:00 P.M. - 4:00 P.M.

8. For which laborer and for what block of time would it be MOST appropriate to schedule the air conditioner cleaning? 8.____

   A. Gearring - 12:30 P.M. - 1:30 P.M.
   B. Blackburn - 11:30 A.M. - 12:30 P.M.
   C. Rogers - 10:00 A.M. - 11:00 A.M.
   D. Gearring - 4:00 P.M. - 5:00 P.M.

9. For which laborer and for what block of time would it be BEST to schedule the pickup of hardware at the supply depot? 9.____

   A. Gearring - 10:30 A.M. - 11:30 A.M.
   B. Blackburn - 11:00 A.M. - 12:30 P.M.
   C. Rogers - 10:30 A.M. - 12:00 Noon
   D. Blackburn - 2:00 P.M. - 3:00 P.M.

10. After all of the work has been scheduled for May 5, which one of the following blocks of time remains unscheduled? 10.____

    A. Rogers - 10:30 A.M. - 11:30 A.M.
    B. Blackburn - 11:30 A.M. - 12:30 P.M.
    C. Gearring - 11:30 A.M. - 12:00 Noon
    D. Rogers - 12:30 P.M. - 1:00 P.M.

Questions 11-20.

DIRECTIONS: Questions 11 through 20 are to be answered solely on the basis of the following chart. Note that each driver works a 9 A.M. to 5 P.M. shift, and is allowed one hour for lunch each day.

SCHEDULE OF PICKUPS AND DELIVERIES
April 12

Driver	Activity	Items	Location	Activity Time Start End	Odometer Reading Start End
McCoy	Pickup	87 refrigerators	163 Bway, N.Y.C.	9:00 12:30	27,328
	Pickup	17 desks	80 Park Ave. So., N.Y.C.	1:30 2:45	
	Pickup	178 chairs	235 E. 43 St. N.Y.C.	2:45 4:15	27,361
Hafner	Delivery	Oak paneling 50 sheets 11' x 15'	4309 Van Cortlandt Pkwy, Bronx	9:00 11:00	15,019
	Pickup	50 desks	4309 Van Cortlandt Pkwy, Bronx	11:00 12:15	
	Delivery	20 glass partitions 5' x 7 1/2'	1059 Murdock Ave., Bronx	1:15 3:45	15,067
O'Neil	Delivery	30 shelves 2' x 4'	605 Lafayette St., Bklyn	9:00 10:45	32,546
	Delivery	17 file cabinets	54 Boerum St. Bklyn	10:45 1:15	
	Pickup	42 desks	430 Fulton St., Bklyn	2:15 4:25	32,575
Tobin	Delivery	37 chairs	809 Kingston Ave., Bklyn	9:00 10:50	33,489
	Delivery	20 sheets 1/2" plywood 4' x 8'	1072 Bedford Ave., Bklyn	10:50 12:20	
	Delivery	15 glass partitions 5' x 7 1/2'	195 Wilson Ave., Bklyn	1:20 3:20	33,510
Guzman	Pickup	20 glass partitions 6' x 7'	135 Barclay St., N.Y.C.	9:00 11:45	12,967
	Pickup	oak paneling 30 sheets 11' x 15'	192 Varick St., N.Y.C.	11:45 1:15	
	Pickup	10 file cabinets	72 Pine St., N.Y.C.	2:15 4:00	13,004

11. The average amount of time spent by O'Neil on each of his activities was APPROXIMATELY _____ hour(s) _____ minutes.

    A. 1; 45   B. 2; 10   C. 2; 45   D. 3; 10

12. At which one of the following locations was the latest pickup started?

    A. 430 Fulton St., Brooklyn
    B. 72 Pine Street, N.Y.C.
    C. 195 Wilson Avenue, Brooklyn
    D. 235 East 43rd Street, N.Y.C.

13. Which one of the following activities was Tobin performing at 11:00 A.M.?

    A. Picking up chairs   B. Delivering glass partitions
    C. Picking up desks   D. Delivering plywood sheets

14. The name of the driver who picked up material and delivered material at the same location is 14.____

    A. McCoy   B. Hafner   C. O'Neil   D. Tobin

15. The name of the driver who picked up 20 glass partitions is 15.____

    A. McCoy   B. Hafner   C. Tobin   D. Guzman

16. According to the chart, the driver who traveled the GREATEST number of miles is 16.____

    A. McCoy   B. Hafner   C. O'Neil   D. Guzman

17. According to the chart, which activities were among those performed by Hafner? He 17.____

    A. picked up 50 sheets of oak paneling and delivered 50 desks
    B. picked up 20 glass partitions and delivered 50 desks
    C. delivered 50 desks and 20 glass partitions
    D. delivered 50 sheets of oak paneling and 20 glass partitions

18. According to the chart, which drivers began their lunch hours after 1:00 P.M.? 18.____

    A. McCoy and Hafner   B. Hafner and O'Neil
    C. O'Neil and Guzman   D. Tobin and Guzman

19. The average number of miles traveled by all trucks on April 12 is MOST NEARLY 19.____

    A. 33   B. 34   C. 37   D. 39

20. According to the chart, which driver spent the GREATEST period of time on a single activity? 20.____

    A. Tobin   B. Guzman   C. Hafner   D. McCoy

KEY(CORRECT ANSWERS)

1.	D	11.	B
2.	A	12.	D
3.	A	13.	D
4.	B	14.	B
5.	D	15.	D
6.	B	16.	B
7.	D	17.	D
8.	D	18.	C
9.	C	19.	B
10.	C	20.	D

TEST 2

DIRECTIONS: Each question or incomplete statement is followed by several suggested answers or completions. Select the one that BEST answers the question or completes the statement. *PRINT THE LETTER OF THE CORRECT ANSWER IN THE SPACE AT THE RIGHT.*

Questions 1-10.

DIRECTIONS: Questions 1 through 10 are based upon equipment and articles. These are items which a foreman may be called upon to move between two distant locations. There are many considerations that govern the correct handling and moving of these articles and, depending upon the characteristics of the individual item, usually there will be one factor that will have the greatest influence on the decision as to how the item is to be handled, the equipment that might be needed, the time of delivery, or the number of employees needed to complete the task satisfactorily.
For each question, select the one choice which represents the factor that should require PRIMARY consideration.

1. The PRIMARY factor to be considered when moving 100 automotive maintenance work tables is:

    A. Can these articles be disassembled?
    B. What is the monetary cost of each table?
    C. How durable is each table?
    D. Are the tables in used or new condition?

2. The PRIMARY factor to be considered when moving tables with folding legs is the

    A. number of tables to be moved
    B. time each laborer takes to fold the set of pairs of legs under each table
    C. use to be made of the tables
    D. value of each table

3. The PRIMARY factor to be considered when moving 200 chairs is the

    A. capability to stack one chair upon another
    B. practicability of disassembling each chair into component parts
    C. special wrapping required for each chair
    D. physical strength required of the movers

4. The PRIMARY factor to be considered when moving 25 swivel chairs is the

    A. knowledge that the frame is of steel construction
    B. identification or labeling of each chair
    C. physical condition of the material on each chair
    D. condition of the casters on each chair

5. The PRIMARY factor to be considered when moving fans is the

    A. requirement that the fans be in operating condition before delivery takes place
    B. fact that replacements are difficult to obtain in cases of loss in shipment

C. fact that the size and bulk of the fan can be accommodated by available transport vehicles
D. absence of wire guards around the fan blades which constitutes a safety hazard

6. The PRIMARY factor to be considered when moving 35 gate valves is the 6._____

   A. past experience that the men assigned have had in moving other kinds of metal equipment
   B. size and weight of each valve
   C. number of forms the foreman must complete
   D. probable use by the mechanic at the site

7. The PRIMARY factor to be considered when moving 100 lockers from storage to a school gym is: 7._____

   A. Can the lockers be disassembled?
   B. Are the lockers to be installed in multiples of 3 units or in multiples of 6 units?
   C. Are the lockers new or used?
   D. What is the scrap value of lockers?

8. The PRIMARY factor to be considered when moving typewriters is the 8._____

   A. provision whether the typewriters are going to be sold or put into storage
   B. determination by the foreman as to what parts are likely to be bent or thrown out of order in the process of moving
   C. cost of replacement parts in the event of damage to the typewriters
   D. type of typewriter; is it manual or electric?

9. The PRIMARY factor to be considered when moving a compressor is the 9._____

   A. absence of a guard enclosing the moving parts of the compressor
   B. degree of close attention the foreman must devote to directing the process of moving
   C. operating instructions furnished by the manufacturer of the compressor
   D. physical dimensions and weight of the compressor

10. The PRIMARY factor to be considered when moving file cabinets from one room to another on the same floor is: 10._____

    A. Can the cabinets be locked?
    B. Are the cabinets letter or legal size?
    C. How many drawers are in each file cabinet?
    D. What is the total number of file cabinets to be moved?

Questions 11-13.

DIRECTIONS: A foreman is asked to write a report on the incident described in the following passage. Answer Questions 11 through 13 based on the following information.

On March 10, Henry Moore, a laborer, was in the process of transferring some equipment from the machine shop to the third floor. He was using a dolly to perform this task and, as he was wheeling the material through the machine shop, laborer Bob Greene called to him. As Henry turned to respond to Bob, he jammed the dolly into Larry Mantell's leg, knocking Larry down in the process and causing the heavy drill that Larry was holding to fall on Larry's foot. Larry started rubbing his foot and then, infuriated, jumped up and punched Henry in the jaw. The force of the blow drove Henry's head back against the wall. Henry did not fight back; he appeared to be dazed. An ambulance was called to take Henry to the hospital, and the ambulance attendant told the foreman that it appeared likely that Henry had suffered a concussion. Larry's injuries consisted of some bruises, but he refused medical attention.

11. An adequate report of the above incident should give as minimum information the names of the persons involved, the names of the witnesses, the date and the time that each event took place, and the   11.____

   A. names of the ambulance attendants
   B. names of all the employees working in the machine shop
   C. location where the accident occurred
   D. nature of the previous safety training each employee had been given

12. The only one of the following which is NOT a fact is: 12.____

   A. Bob called to Henry
   B. Larry suffered a concussion
   C. Larry rubbed his foot
   D. The incident took place in the machine shop

13. Which of the following would be the MOST accurate summary of the incident for the foreman to put in his report of the accident?   13.____

   A. Larry Mantell punched Henry Moore because a drill fell on his foot and he was angry. Then Henry fell and suffered a concussion.
   B. Henry Moore accidentally jammed a dolly into Larry Mantell's foot, knocking Larry down. Larry punched Henry, pushing him into the wall and causing him to bang his head against the wall.
   C. Bob Greene called Henry Moore. A dolly then jammed into Larry Mantell and knocked him down. Larry punched Henry who tripped and suffered some bruises. An ambulance was called.
   D. A drill fell on Larry Mantell's foot. Larry jumped up suddenly and punched Henry Moore and pushed him into the wall. Henry may have suffered a concussion as a result of falling.

14. It is said that the morale of a staff is usually a good indication of the quality of leadership exercised by the supervisor of the staff. Of the following, the BEST indication of high morale among a staff is: 14.____

   A. Disciplinary actions against members of the staff are rare
   B. It is seldom necessary for the staff to work overtime
   C. The staff is seldom late in reporting for work
   D. The staff subordinates personal desires in favor of group objectives

15. In starting a work simplification study, the one of the following steps that should be taken FIRST is to   15.____

   A. break the work down into its elements
   B. draw up a chart of operations

C. enlist the interest and cooperation of the personnel
D. suggest alternative procedures

16. Of the following, the MOST important value of a manual of procedures is that it USUALLY   16._____

    A. eliminates the need for on-the-job training
    B. decreases the span of control which can be exercised by individual supervisory personnel
    C. outlines methods of operation for ready reference
    D. provides concrete examples of work previously performed by employees

17. In conducting an analysis of the flow of work in a store-roori or storehouse, it is USUALLY advisable to begin the analysis with the   17._____

    A. supervisory work
    B. technical work
    C. work of a major routine nature
    D. work of a minor routine nature

18. When planning a staff development program for his subordinates, the one of the following which it is usually MOST important for the foreman to consider is the   18._____

    A. chief storekeeping problems of the department
    B. common needs of his subordinates in terms of the daily work situation
    C. evaluation of similar training programs offered by other departments
    D. time available for classes and meetings

19. Reprimanding a subordinate when he has done something wrong should be done PRIMARILY in order to   19._____

    A. deter others from similar acts
    B. improve the subordinate's future performance
    C. maintain discipline
    D. uphold departmental rules

20. You find that delivery of a certain item cannot possibly be nade to a using agency by the date the using agency requested. Of the following, the MOST advisable course of action for you to take FIRST is to   20._____

    A. cancel the order and inform the using agency
    B. discuss the problem with the using agency
    C. notify the using agency to obtain the item through direct purchase
    D. schedule the delivery for the earliest possible date

KEY (CORRECT ANSWERS)

1.	A	11.	C
2.	A	12.	B
3.	A	13.	B
4.	D	14.	D
5.	C	15.	C
6.	B	16.	C
7.	A	17.	C
8.	B	18.	B
9.	D	19.	B
10.	D	20.	B

THE FOREMAN
BASIC FUNDAMENTALS OF SUPERVISION AND MANAGEMENT

CONTENTS

	Page
I. THE JOB OF THE FOREMAN	1
His Duties and Responsibilities	1
Human Relations Duties	1
Training Duties	1
Production Duties	1
1. Schedules	1
2. Quality	2
3. Costs	2
4. General Production Duties	2
His Authority	2
1. Supervision	2
2. Use of Productive Facilities	2
3. Maintenance of Quality	2
4. Control of jobs	2
Special Problems of the Foreman in a Small Plant	3
II. BASIC RESPONSIBILITIES	3
Getting Production Out on Time	3
1. Materials	4
2. Schedule Balance	4
3. Work Simplification	4
4. Machine Utilization	4
5. Worker Utilization	4
Maintaining Quality Standards	5
Holding Production Costs Down	5
1. Direct Labor Costs	7
2. Indirect Labor Costs	7
3. Material Utilization	8
4. Machine Utilization	8
5. Methods Improvement	8
How Top Management Can Help Foremen Improve Efficiency	9
III. THE FOREMAN'S TRAINING FUNCTION	9
Training New Employees	9
1. Explaining Company Policies	10
2. Instruction Covering Shop Operations	10
3. Coaching Covering the Job of a New Employee	10

	Training Employees Promoted to New Jobs		10
	Training an Understudy		10
	Other Training Responsibilities		11
	1.	Orientation of Salesmen and Other Company Personnel	11
	2.	Special Training Sessions for Employees	11

IV. **THE FOREMAN'S PERSONAL RELATIONSHIPS AND CONTACTS** — 11
    Relationships With Workers — 11
    Contacts With Supervisors in Other Departments — 12
    Relationships With Superiors — 12
    Contacts With Unions and Union Officials — 12
    Contacts With the Public — 13

V. **DEVELOPING BETTER FOREMEN** — 13
    Qualifications Which Foremen Need — 13
        1. Leadership Ability — 14
        2. Organizing Ability — 14
        3. Character — 14
        4. Judgment — 14
        5. Technical Skill and Mechanical Skill — 14
        6. Education — 14
        7. Initiative — 15
        8. Human Interest — 15
        9. Physical and Mental Requirements — 15
    Finding Prospects — 15
    What Kind of Training — 15
    Solving the Problem in Small Plants — 16
        1. Cooperation With Other Small Plants — 16
        2. Cooperation With Colleges and Universities — 16
        3. Use of Programs Developed By Larger Companies — 16
        4. Use of Supervisory Programs Developed by Management Associations — 17
    Measuring the Results — 17
    How Top Management Promotes Foreman Development — 18
        1. Incentive Payments — 18
        2. Authority — 18
        3. Prestige — 18

CONCISE TEXT
THE FOREMAN
BASIC FUNDAMENTALS OF SUPERVISION AND MANAGEMENT

I. THE JOB OF THE FOREMAN

- **His duties and responsibilities**
- **His authority**
- **Special problems of the foreman in a small plant**

A foreman is the member of plant management who has been delegated the authority to manage a shop, a function, or a department. He is the one whom the folks in the shop call boss; he is the one they look to for instructions and supervision; and he shoulders the responsibility for all work done by those who report to him. In short, he is the first line of management. In this position he is a key figure both as a production manager and in the plant's relationships with its employees.

His Duties and Responsibilities

The foreman's job is to use the men, machines, and material assigned to him for the purpose of getting out production under conditions specified by his superiors. In order to accomplish this objective, he has to perform a multitude of duties and responsibilities.

Human Relations Duties

1. To maintain good relationships with employees, with other departments in the plant, with his superiors, with customers, with unions, and with the public.
2. To settle grievances—one of his most important duties.
3. To be familiar with the union contract if there is one, and to run the shop in strict accordance with it.
4. To be familiar with company policies and interpret them to the workers as management has explained them to him
5. To exercise leadership and supervision over the people assigned to him.
6. To develop and maintain job interest among his employees.
7. To be available when those who report to him need help or assistance, whether it be of a business or personal nature.

Training Duties

1. To inform new employees assigned to him about company policies.
2. To see that new employees receive adequate job instruction.
3. To train an understudy who can take his place in the event he is absent, or is promoted, or resigns.

Production Duties:

1. Schedules: He is expected to get the production out in accordance with schedules prescribed by his superiors; to coordinate the various activities in his department for

---

*n.b. Pronouns are used collectively

the purpose of eliminating delays and bottlenecks; and to see that the men, materials, and machines assigned to him are fully utilized.
2. Quality: He is expected to protect the customer from the receipt of faulty products through proper shop precautions.
3. Costs: He is expected to keep production costs within the budget approved by his superiors
4. General Production Duties: He is expected to be constantly alert to new methods and procedures which will improve quality, reduce delays, and reduce production costs; he is also expected to see that all production activities conform with plant safety regulations.

Although the duties of a foreman vary by necessity from plant to plant, the ones listed above cover the basic responsibilities which most foreman are expected to shoulder.

His Authority

A foreman's authority to make decisions and take action is delegated to him by his superiors. While this, too, must of necessity vary according to the circumstances, most foreman have the following general types of authority.

1. Supervision: This involves the authority to exercise full supervision over the men, materials, machines, and supplies assigned to his department—within the limits of company policies.
2. Use of Productive Facilities: This involves the authority to requisition materials, supplies, and personnel and incur certain other expenses within the limits of his approved budget.
3. Maintenance of Quality: This involves the authority to reject any item produced in his shop which falls in his opinion to meet standards of quality as prescribed by his superiors.
4. Control of Jobs: This involves, for some foremen, the authority to hire and fire.

A foreman's influence is often greater than his specific authority. In certain areas, his superior may regard him as a personal representative, and by virtue of that fact, the foreman's recommendations carry considerable weight. For example, his recommendations concerning personnel, product design, the need for more shop space, new production processes or formulas, and new equipment are given careful consideration. He is usually closer to problems of this nature than any other official in the plant. In the eyes of the workers, the foreman's authority within the shop is all inclusive. If by chance the workers have any question on this score, it is only because the foreman's superiors fail to back him up adequately.

In exercising his authority, and in accepting responsibilities, the foreman acts as a member of a team, the management team. But as in any kind of team work, he must also rely upon his superiors for advice, guidance, and information. Likewise, his superiors are dependent on him for information and suggestions. Crystallizing this concept of teamwork in the minds of all members of management is perhaps the greatest single element of help that can be given to foremen. It encourages greater cooperation between the foreman's shop and other departments, and as a result, the whole company benefits from it. In addition, the foreman needs the cooperation and support of every department with which he comes in contact if he is to do his job effectively.

Special Problems of the Foreman in a Small Plant

The problems of a foreman in a small plant are often different from those of a foreman in a large company. There are two basic reasons why this is true.

First, small plants can't always afford the services of those specialized departments which are accepted as an essential part of the organization in a large plant. For example, relatively few small plants enjoy the benefit of time-study specialists, of full-time production inspectors, or of separate machine maintenance departments. Although such services may not be handled by specialized personnel, the work still has to be done, and quite often the responsibility for doing it is assigned to the foreman. As a result, the duties and problems of small-plant foremen are usually broader in scope than are those of foremen in a larger plant.

Second, a small plant typically operates on a more intimate basis than a large one. Thus, the relationships between department heads are more personal, and as a result everybody gets to know everybody else much better than is possible in a larger plant. Similarly, department heads are more dependent upon each other for cooperation and help. In such a situation, the foreman has to be doubly alert to the value of good personal relationships, because one unfortunate experience with just one department head in the plant can create a problem between himself and the heads of several other departments. If such an incident occurs, and it results in less cooperation between his shop and other departments, his value to the company is greatly diminished. For this reason the foreman must be an accepted member of the small plant family, in fact as well as theory, or else he has no place in the organization. Therefore, the smaller the plant, the more important personal relationships become.

II. BASIC RESPONSIBILITIES OF A FOREMAN

The foreman has three basic responsibilities: Getting production out on time, getting production to conform with quality standards, and getting production out at the least possible cost.

Unless a foreman can satisfy these three responsibilities, he is unable to live up to the requirements of his job.

Getting Production Out on Time

The foreman's department has to satisfy certain production quotas because customers want to receive their purchases within a certain period of time. In order to make sure that customers get their shipments within the time specified, one of the foreman's superiors usually develops a production schedule in consultation with the foreman, the sales department, and other interested departments. This schedule then becomes a timetable to which operations must be gear. It places a maximum limit on the amount of time that can be allowed to produce a given number of units. The foreman's objective, insofar as schedules are concerned, should not only be to get production out on schedule, but to get it put as much ahead of schedule as possible, within the resources of his department.

In meeting schedule deadlines, a foreman needs to maintain a set of figures which will tell him at the end of each day how his shop is producing. These figures should tell him that the shop is either adequately or inadequately organized for getting the work out on time. Without such information, his ability to meet schedules is left up to chance.

For example, if a schedule calls for the production of 220 units in a 30-day month, the foreman knows that his shop has 22 work days in which to do the job required. When, during any given day, less than 10 units are produced, he knows he is falling behind schedule and can take remedial action before the production deadline arrives. The foreman's superiors are also interested in these figures and he has a responsibility to keep them posted at all times as to the progress in relation to the scheduled requirement.

Sometimes production falls behind schedule for reasons which have to be referred to higher authority for correction. For example, shipments of raw materials which are needed to produce the finished product may be delayed by the supplier; abnormal sickness may require overtime by others and approval to thus add to expenses; or a machine breaks down and delay production to such an extent that the schedule has to be revised.

However, most of the reasons for a shop falling behind schedule are due to internal conditions. Ingenuity of the foreman in identifying the causes and taking remedial action is a test of his ability to hold down the job of foreman. Some of the most common conditions which lie within the authority of the foreman to correct are as follows:

1. Materials: The material which goes into the production process may be located in an inconvenient spot. It may be placed where it is so inaccessible or located so far away from the workers that must valuable production time is lost in transporting the material to the machines. Frequently, a more efficient arrangement of materials will solve the production lag problem. The foreman has to be alert to the need for having raw materials placed in the best location.

2. Schedule Balance: Oftentimes the workers engaged in producing a certain part of the product will get ahead of those who are producing other parts. This leaves workers who turn out the finished items standing idle until the parts from the lagging operations shop are available. Since all parts of a given product must be produced on schedule, if the deadline for completed units is to be met, the foreman often has to redistribute the number of men and machines assigned to a given phase of the operation in order to maintain the proper balance of output between the various operations being performed.

3. Work Simplification: Sometimes the number of operations performed by each worker are so great or so unrelated that the rate of production is slowed down. In such a case production can be speeded up if the job of each worker is broken down so that he has a smaller variety of steps to perform. Frequently, depending upon the nature of the produce being produced, this saves time because it reduces the motions of changing from one operation to another. This is a possibility the foreman has to consider, for often it is the key to quicker production.

4. Machine Utilization: Scheduling the work in proper sequence and with balanced timing is essential if the foreman expects to get maximum use out of each available machine. Regular inspection and maintenance of each machine is also essential if disruptive breakdowns are to be avoided. Down time is expensive. It adds to production costs, to say nothing of the cost of the investment in equipment.

5. Worker Utilization: Placing workers on those phases of the operation where they can do most effective work is also an aid to meeting production schedules. The foreman has to know how much work each employee is producing, and how his production compares with those around him in order that the slow ones may be singled out for consultation. A worker who is a laggard on one job may do better work on other jobs for which he is better adapted.

In order to meet production requirement, a foreman must maintain a delicate balance between men, the machines, and the materials in his shop. Failure to maintain the balance will result in disrupted production and eventual failure to meet the scheduled deadline.

Maintaining Quality Standards

Production has to conform with quality standards as prescribed by top management because the customer will return any unit which fails to meet those standards. If such returns reach significant proportions, the reputation and prestige of the plant suffers. Because of the embarrassment arising from the sale of faulty good to customers, most plants have an arrangement whereby finished goods are inspected before they are shipped to the customer. If, upon inspection, it is found that the product meets all quality standards, it is approved for shipment. If it doesn't, it is rejected and sent back to the shop for more attention. The practice of conducting such inspections is commonly referred to as "quality control." Some plants, especially those which produce critical items (such as parachutes), inspect every unit before it is "o.k.'d." But this is expensive, and hence other plants use a type of statistical quality control. This is a system whereby only one unit out of a given number of units is checked, with the assumption that if the units checked are found all right, then those in between are likewise all right. The system is becoming more popular in plants and is proving to be effective.

The ideal arrangement is to have finished production inspected by someone who reports to the foreman's superior. This is desirable because the inspector is checking work which the foreman is responsible for producing, and a person who has no responsibility to the foreman, or who has had no part in the production of the items can usually be more objective in his inspections. However, in some of the smaller plant, when inspectors are not carried on the payroll, the inspection function may be delegated to the foreman himself.

Under either arrangement, the foreman should maintain the following information concerning units which are rejected, for use in improving the quality of production.

1. The number of units rejected within the plant each day, week, or month (whichever is most practicable.).
2. The number of units rejected by customers each day, week, or month.
3. The name of the worker who produced the unit, if such information is available.

The inspector should keep both the foreman and his superiors advised of the number of units rejected by him. The foreman's superiors should keep the foreman and the inspector advised regarding the number of units rejected by the customers. These records should be used by all three parties to determine whether the number of rejections is excessive. If the number of units rejected exceeds the average rate, it is then up to the foreman to check with the employees responsible and reanalyze his procedures to determine what corrective action is necessary. However, even though the number of rejections is below normal, the foreman still has a responsibility to devise ways and means of effecting further reductions. The best foremen have the lowest rejection rates.

Holding Production Costs Down

The use of shop budgets for cost control purposes is the most effective means for making the foreman cost conscious. This is true because he knows that he either has to live within his budget or explain the reasons why. In many plants, the cost accountant prepares a monthly report showing detailed types of expenses as charged to each department in relation to the amount budgeted. This report is useful to top management because it tells how effectively the foreman has controlled his expenses during the previous month. It also serves as a useful supervisory tool for the foreman because it tells him what particular expenditure exceeded the budget, which enables him to know in which area remedial action is necessary.

However, if the foreman is to operate his department as effectively as possible, he can't wait until the end of the month to see how good its performance has been. He usually needs to know on the following day how well he did the day before; in other words, he needs daily expense figures which he can compare with daily budget figures. Such figures on a rounded basis can be easily developed by the foreman himself. All he needs to do is take the previous month's budget report and develop from it average daily budget figures which will give him a fairly good idea of what his maximum daily expenses for the current month should be. He can then develop an estimate on the following day which will tell him what his approximate costs were on the previous day. By comparing the previous day's estimate with his estimated daily expense budget he can get a fairly good idea of how well his expenses are being controlled. If accurate daily performance records can be developed, they of course are more desirable than estimated figures. But many small plants do not have the resources for keeping detailed expense records on a daily basis.

The budget covering the foreman's shop should be prepared by the foreman himself. This not only accentuates the importance of the foreman's responsibility, but it is a more realistic way of preparing a budget. The foreman is closer to the needs of his department than anyone else and if the budget is prepared by someone farther removed from the shop activities, it cannot be all-inclusive and will usually result in the foreman asking for authority to exceed the budget because something was overlooked when it was originally set up. If, after the foreman prepares the budget, his superiors want to cut some of the estimated costs, they then have a more realistic set of figures from which they can estimate what adjustments should be made.

Once a foreman's budget has been established, he should clearly understand that he is expected to keep his expenditures within budgetary limitations. Authority to exceed the budgeted amount should be granted only upon the specific request of the foreman, and only after it has been determined how far he should exceed the budget and for what type of expenditure.

A good foreman not only wants to keep within his budget, he wants to keep his expenditures as far below the budget as possible because he wants to be a good enough administrator to get the production out with the least possible cost.

A budget report to be effectively used as a means of controlling expenditures in the shop should be issued in final form by the accounting people once a month. It should show both the actual and budgeted monthly expense for the following items:

1. Direct labor costs
2. Indirect labor costs
3. Material cost
4. Maintenance costs
5. Costs of supplies, including tools
6. Light, heat, power, and telephone cost

These are controllable costs (some, of course, are more controllable than others) which the foreman should be conscious of at all times. Other items of a non-controllable nature are also usually included in the budget report. However, as long as the foreman gets reports covering his controllable expenses, he has something which he can use to guide him in his efforts to run a more efficient shop.

The foreman has to be continually conscious of the cost which results from everything that goes on in the shop. Here is a list of some of the major areas on which a foreman has to keep a particularly watchful eye if he is to successfully hold expenses down:

1. Direct Labor Costs: You don't normally cut costs by cuffing wages because lower wages attract less efficient people and in the long run, a wage cut increases labor costs. In fact, some shops have been known to cut costs by raising wages, because through higher wages they were able to attract more efficient people. As a result, fewer people were needed to turn out the production. The real personnel costs that can and must be controlled are those resulting from absenteeism, turnover, accidents, and improper utilization of workers.

    A worker who is guilty of excessive absenteeism increases shop costs because the work schedule of the shop has to be readjusted each time he is absent. That costs money. This is a matter which should be ironed out on a personal basis between the employee and the foreman on the merits of each case.

    Excessive turnover is also costly. It is costly in terms of the time and effort used (a) to find and process replacements; (b) to train new employees to your equipment and your methods. Furthermore, it is costly in terms of productivity; it is usually several weeks or longer before the performance of new employees equals that of your experienced workers. The problem of excessive turnover can, in many cases, be clarified by getting from each employee the reasons for his leaving. Both the foreman and the personnel department should be interested in such information. Once the true reasons for turnover are known, corrective action can be taken. High turnover is frequently caused by poor selection, low wages, or poor supervision on the part of the foreman.

    When a worker is incapacitated because of an occupational accident, not only does the company temporarily lose his services, but hospital bills, increased workmen's compensation assessments, increased insurance rates, and law suit are apt to result. While not all of these charges would be reflected in the foreman's budget, nevertheless hospital charge and other miscellaneous items become a part of his labor costs.

    Failure by the foreman to utilize fully the time an employee is on the job results in increased production costs not only because the worker is being paid for time he has not worked, but because failure to use the regular man-hours available may force the foreman to resort to overtime work in order to get production out on time. A foreman should organize the next day's work before he leaves the shop at night. This is the best way to assure full utilization of all employees.

2. Indirect Labor Costs: These are the labor costs which have nothing to do with actual manufacturing or production costs, such as the cost of labor required sweeping the floors, and repairing the machines. In order to keep indirect labor costs to a minimum, the foreman will do well to keep his eye on two major items: the cost of maintaining machines and the cost of handling raw materials. In small plants especially, responsibility for the costs of these functions falls upon the production foreman.

    Experience proves that it is cheaper to inspect machines at regular intervals and replace worn parts than to wait until they break down. For when a machine breaks down, its repair usually costs more than keeping the machine in good condition through the process of regular inspection. In addition, a broken-down machine disrupts production, which results in even greater expense.

Perhaps one of the most overlooked expense items in the indirect labor category is the cost of materials handling. It has been estimated, for example, that 36 percent of the labor dollar in the electrical industry is spent in moving materials destined to go into the production process from one place to another. When the material arrives at the plant, it is moved into the warehouse. While there it may be moved several times to make room for other incoming shipments. Then it is moved to the shop, where it may be moved again several times before it is finally used in production. Such a procedure not only make indirect labor costs excessively high, but also increases the cost of material because the more the material is moved, the more it is in danger of being damaged.

3. Material Utilization: The foreman can cut the cost of materials by developing standardized procedures for employees to follow in cutting up a piece of material. Most pieces come in standard sizes and lend themselves to formal cutting procedures which can result in considerable savings. A furniture factory, for instance, has found that a piece of plywood which comes in standard 4x8 foot sizes can make a small bookcase with only one-half of a board foot to spare, if the cutting is done in a certain way. If the piece is cut any other way, it takes two such pieces, with a lot of material left over. Most of it cannot be used at all, and the part that is usable can be used only by disrupting the assembly line. Material costs are a big factor in production and proper utilization can help hold production costs down.

4. Machine Utilization: Machines cost money whether they are utilized or not because they depreciate and become obsolete. To justify these costs, machines should be fully utilized at all times through proper work organization. Therefore, before the foreman goes home at night, he should know exactly how every employee and machine will be utilized when the shop opens up the next day.

5. Methods Improvement: To do his job of keeping costs down to a minimum, a foreman must be, in addition to everything else, an "efficiency expert." He must constantly be on the lookout for better, cheaper, and easier ways of getting the production out. He should consider such things as the number of steps a worker must take in going from one operation to another; a rearrangement of equipment will save money if that will cut down on the number of steps required. He needs to consider the number of motions a worker must go through to complete a given operation; if a change in procedure will make some motions unnecessary, he has saved the company money.

In attempting to make his shop as efficient as possible, the foreman can make progress if he will look to his employees for ideas. They are in a position to see many things which he is either unable or too busy to see. Some of the best ideas for increasing efficiency in plants come from employee. A formalized suggestion plan promoted by the foremen will serve as a stimulus for employees to develop new ideas and turn them in. A suggestion plan if properly promoted can be one of the most effective steps toward greater plant efficiency.

How Top Management Can Help Foremen Improve Efficiency

There are at least three things which top management can do which will help the foreman improve the efficiency of his shop:

1. Let him have a voice in the purchase of materials, tools, and equipment: The foreman lives every day with the materials, tools, and equipment in his department. He knows the good and bad points of every brand-name in his shop. He knows which items speed up production and which ones do not. While there is no need to give the foreman the last word on purchases made for his shop, he should be given the opportunity to express his opinions on the matter. In most cases, he will be able to offer ideas that will influence the type of purchases to be made. This should result in having more efficient equipment and in improved morale of the work force.

2. Let him select his own employees: Recruiting of personnel should be done through the personnel office, based upon qualifications submitted by the foreman. But the foreman should have the authority to determine which of the applicants submitted by the personnel office he wants to have in his department. This enables the foreman to select those people whom he feels will be most capable of doing the job the way he wants it done. Such an arrangement is conducive to a more harmonious shop, and helps give the foreman the prestige necessary to carry out his responsibility. The personnel office should continue to make personnel policies to which the foreman should of course conform, but a foreman should have the freedom to select his own employees within the limit of those policies.

3. Give the foreman authority to recommend or deny wage increases: If the foreman wants to have the wage of one of his employees raised, he should have the authority to recommend the increase. Moreover, every effort should be made to grant it, provided it does not conflict with the plant's overall personnel policies. This procedure helps also to increase the prestige of the foreman and gives the workers assurance that their ability to get wage increases is not dependent solely upon some higher authority who is unfamiliar with their work. Conversely, if the worker's performance does not, in the opinion of the foreman, justify a proposed wage increase, he should be authorized to deny it. If the plant is a union shop, of course, suitable adjustments in these policies would have to be made.

III. THE FOREMAN'S TRAINING FUNCTIONS

A foreman has to assume certain training functions—whether the plant has a training department or not because there are certain procedures and techniques which are peculiar to many jobs. In a small plant, it is often difficult for anyone outside of the department in question to be entirely familiar with its procedures and techniques. Moreover, procedural changes often take place so fast that a centralized training department would find it almost impossible to keep on a current basis.

Training New Employees

The foreman has a threefold training responsibility for new employees:

1. Explaining company policies: He has a responsibility, at the time the new employee reports for work, to brief him on all company policies which directly relate to him individually; for example: regulations regarding pay, including lost time and overtime, seniority provisions, seniority increases, union contract provisions, and promotions; company-sponsored insurance plans; workmen's compensation, and the rights of the employee in connection with each. These are items of such importance to the new employee that they are an essential part of his orientation.

2. Instruction covering shop operations: The foreman also has a responsibility to introduce the new employee around the shop, explain the functions of each worker, point out the different types of equipment and what they are used for, and explain shop safety regulations. He also should explain the relationship of the new employee's job to the rest of the department and to the rest of the company, and briefly outline the organization of the company as a whole. This helps the employee to get a proper perspective of his new job and the plant.

3. Coaching covering the job of a new employee: The foreman has a responsibility to see that the new employee is properly broken in on his new job. This is usually done by assigning him to an experienced employee who provides detailed instruction and assistance until the new worker is qualified to handle his assignments alone.

When a new employee is hired for a complicated job requiring several different types of operations, foremen frequently break the job done into a series of simple steps, to facilitate training. When the new employee learns how to handle the first operation, he is then instructed on how to do the second operation until he has mastered that step, and so on. This is known as the "job dilution" type of training. It was widely used in shops both large and small during World War II. This method of breaking in a new employee on a complicated job usually accelerate the training period with a minimum of effort.

Training Employees Promoted to New Jobs

When an employee is promoted or transferred to a different job, the foreman has a responsibility to see that adequate instruction is given the worker on his new job until he is qualified to handle his assignments alone. As in the case of a newly hired employee, such training usually requires that an experienced employee provide the necessary detailed instruction.

Training an Understudy

The foreman has a responsibility to develop an understudy who can take over his job if and when he is promoted or leaves the company.

Some men hesitate to develop an understudy because they feel he may eventually prove to be a competitor for the job of foreman. Yet a foreman owes it to himself to have an understudy who can take his place. Failure to have one may prevent him from being promoted to a better job, simply because there is no one to take his place. In many cases, an oversight of this nature has stood in the way of a foreman's promotion.

From the plant manager's viewpoint, an understudy is desirable because of the possibility that the foreman may get sick, leave the company, or be eligible for transfer or promotion.

Other Training Responsibilities

Foremen are often given other types of training responsibilities, among which are the following:

1. Orientation of Salesmen and Other Company Personnel: Foremen are often called upon to explain the production process to salesmen for their information in selling the product to customers. Others in the company who hold management positions often call upon the foreman to give them the same briefing so they can get a more complete picture of plant operations. Sometimes foremen are called upon to explain the production process to customers who want to know how the product they buy is made.

2. Special Training Sessions for Employees: When major changes are made in the production process, plant mechanization is increased, wage payment systems are changed, time-study plans are introduced, plant operations are reorganized, or special sales and advertising campaigns are initiated., the foreman has a responsibility to explain to his employees the reasons why the changes are taking place, and how these changes will affect them.

Some plant, realizing that the foreman is the company so far as his employees are concerned, rely upon him to hold employee training sessions in cooperation with other supervisors for the purpose of acquainting employees with the operations of the company in general, why it operates the way it does, what the plant balance sheet shows, what the current business conditions are and how they affect the operations of the company, and what the prospects of the company are for the future. Such sessions help to educate the worker with respect to economics and the free enterprise system. Most research organizations agree that employees are in need of such training because many of them are often ill-informed on matters of this nature.

IV. THE FOREMAN'S PERSONAL RELATIONSHIPS AND CONTACTS

In the average small plant, each function and each department is so interdependent that the foreman who succeeds in establishing good personal relationships throughout the company has a much easier time performing his job. Since the foreman's shop is dependent upon other departments for materials, equipment, supplies, and personnel, the amount of cooperation he is able to get from other departments has a definite effect upon the performance of his shop.

Relationships With Workers

The value of good personal relationships between the foreman and his employees cannot be overestimated, because it is through such relationships that he is able to settle more grievances and avert more union complaints than any other member of the management team. A foreman in one small plant, for example, is known to have settled an average of one grievance a month for the past 5 years. His technique is simple. He listens until the worker gets the complaint off his chest. Then, if the worker is upset at the time the complaint is made, he waits until the next day, when the subject can be discussed more objectively. If after investigation he finds that the complaint is valid, he takes corrective action provided his department is at fault. If another department is at fault, such as the payroll or personnel office, he request the department in question to take corrective action. And he follows up on the matter until the case is closed.

If a foreman does not enjoy good personal relationships with his employees, they may not choose to discuss their grievances with him. They may, instead, take them direct to the union and thereby strain the relationship between union and plant before the matter is settled. There is evidence that good foreman-employee relationships have been responsible for smoothing out many grievances which otherwise would have resulted in strikes.

Foremen who enjoy the best personal relationships with their employees are those whose actions prove that they sincerely have the interest of their workers at heart. Such action becomes evident in the foreman's efforts to provide his employees with adequate equipment and supplies; when he tries to make the job easier for them; when he tries to improve their comfort while on the job; when he takes an interest in seeing that they get their paychecks on time and in the right amount; when he makes allowances for illness in the family or other personal difficulties of his workers; and when he tries to promote harmony among all of the people in his department.

Many foremen find that occasional parties after work help to improve morale by enabling everybody to get acquainted. Also, occasional social visits to the homes of his employees improves their job interest and enables the foreman to know them better. If a foreman operates his shop on a strictly impartial basis, visit to the home of his employees are a great help in improving morale.

Contacts With Supervisors in Other Departments

Much that is used within a shop, such as materials and supplies, comes from other departments. The foreman, therefore, has to have the cooperation of these other departments if he is to get from them the kind of service he needs in order to keep his shop running efficiently. While it is true that he can appeal to his superior if the cooperation he wants from other departments is not adequate, this procedure takes time. It creates even worse feelings, and in the long run, the foreman who made the complaint loses more than he gains. There is no substitute for good, spontaneous, interdepartmental cooperation.

Relationships With Superiors

The foreman has a responsibility to keep his superiors informed regarding his problems, his needs and the overall operations of his department. Top management relies on information of this nature for control and planning purposes. He also has a responsibility to keep his superiors currently informed regarding those problems and situations affecting the performance of his shop which are outside the scope of his authority to handle. Failure to keep his superiors properly informed may result in eventual embarrassment to the foreman because a small problem, over which he has no control, may later develop into a major problem if it is allowed to go unattended.

Contacts With Unions and Union Officials

A foreman's contacts with unions and union officials must at all times be honest and sincere. There is no other way to deal effectively with unions. It is a foreman's responsibility to respect and abide by the agreement which his company and his employees' union have developed. The foreman helps to promote better management-labor relations when the union knows that he fully respects and makes a sincere effort to support all provisions of the agreement which his company has signed.

Contacts With the Public

The foreman is often called upon to handle plant tours for groups who want to see how products are manufactured. This places a public relations responsibility upon the foreman to give such visitors a good impression of the plant. Industrial management is becoming more and more aware of the need to acquaint the general public with the facts about its plants and the contributions which they make to the community. One of the more effective ways to do this is through plant tours.

The heads of many plants encourage the foremen and other supervisors to take part as much as possible in civic activities designed to improve the community in which the plant is located. They take the position that since the plant is a part of the community, the leadership in that plant should take a definite interest in community affairs. When the foreman engages in such activities, he not only advertises his company as being a civic-minded organization, but he assumes community responsibilities which contribute to the growth of both himself and the community.

V. DEVELOPING BETTER FOREMEN

The problem of developing better foremen is more than just a matter of putting them through a foremanship training course. In fact, a training program is only one of several factors which have a bearing on the development of foremen. Before there can be effective training, it must first be determined that the foremen and prospective foremen possess the basic qualifications which such a job demands. Any time spent in training people in foremanship is wasted unless those being trained actually have the qualifications necessary to absorb and use such training effectively.

Even then, the maximum effectiveness of a foreman training program cannot be realized unless top management follows up such training with an arrangement which provides proper recognition of the role which a foreman is expected to play in his organization. If a foreman completes training course which stresses the importance of his job (and virtually all foremen training courses do stress this) and later finds that the importance of that job is minimized through lack of proper authority and recognition, part of the value of the training course is lost.

The problem of developing better foremen is, therefore, one which involves three basic considerations: (1) the prospective foreman must be qualified for the job, (2) special training for development on the job should be available, and (3) the importance of the role the foreman is expected to play in the operation of the plant should be fully recognized.

Qualifications Which Foremen Need

The wide publicity given in recent years to the importance of the role played by foremen in industry has developed a realization by top management that, in the eyes of the worker, the foreman is the company, and, in the eyes of the community, the company is judged in part by the impression the foreman makes on the general public. This realization has resulted in a more careful selection of people who are placed in such jobs. Since the foreman is charged with the responsibility of getting the job done in the quickest possible time and with the least possible expense, he must be a highly qualified person. Recent studies by management associations and research organizations generally indicate that top management today is looking for the following nine qualifications in the people who are considered for the position of foreman:

1. Leadership Ability: A recent survey taken among 300 companies indicates that leadership ability is the first qualification that top management looks for in a prospective foreman. The modern concept of a foreman is one who provides leadership, not one who simply gives orders. His ability to get production out on time with the least possible cost is dependent to a large extent upon how effectively his leadership can stimulate job interest and satisfaction on the part of his employees. A foreman is a good leader when his employees turn out a good job not because they have to but because they as employees want to do a good job.

2. Organizing Ability: A foreman has men, machines, and materials assigned to him. He must have the ability to organize all three factors in an orderly, clear-cut, and simplified manner, whenever circumstances demand it. Nothing will break down the morale of a shop quicker than a situation where the work is so poorly organized that the employees are, figuratively, stepping on each other, or where some employees are overworked while others are standing around waiting for work. Unless a foreman has the administrative skill necessary to organize the work of his shop in a manner that will hold bottlenecks and trouble spots to a minimum, his other qualifications as a foreman will be of little value.

3. Character: A foreman has to be honest and fair with his employees at all times. In this respect his reputation must be above reproach. One of the costliest operators a company can have is a foreman or supervisor who arouses suspicion and distrust. Employees will invariably produce less work under such supervision. Their morale will not only be low, but they will spend valuable production time worrying about what the foreman is going to do next. These result in rumors and secret discussions between employees on company time, which increases the time and the cost required to get out production.

4. Judgment: Employees do better work when they have confidence in the foreman's judgment. Especially is this true in a shop where poor judgment could result in accidents to employees. Very often employees are asked to do a job or follow a procedure in which they do not see any merit. Confidence in the judgment of the foreman will tend to allay any fears that the foreman doesn't know what he is doing.

5. Technical Skill and Mechanical Ability: The idea foreman should be able to run any machine in the shop as well if not better than any employee under his supervision. It helps strengthen his position as a leader. However, this is not always possible because some machines cannot be operated at peak efficiency unless a person has daily experience with them. Nevertheless, a foreman should know the capabilities and limitations of every machine in his department and should be able to tell new people how to operate them effectively.

6. Education: While it is true that more and more foremen have had college training, a college education is not regarded as a necessary qualification. Some of the country's best foremen have never been to college. Insofar as education is concerned, top management is looking, first, for foremen whose background provides a broad common sense viewpoint and practical understanding. Although college training helps in the development of these qualities, it is also recognized that such qualities can be the outgrowth of past experience.

7. Initiative: A foreman must be a self-starter. If he is to discharge his responsibility as a manager of a function, he must be capable of taking action necessary to keep production going with only occasional supervision from his superiors. Any foreman who requires constant supervision is not performing the functions of a foreman.

8. Human Interest: A foreman should be interested in all things which affect the wellbeing of his employees. This involves personal as well as shop problems because personal problems frequently affect performance on the job. Moreover, the foreman is, oftentimes, the only person to whom employees can go for counsel and advice on problems of this nature. When a worker knows that the foreman has his personal interest at heart, his morale and job interest are greatly stimulated.

9. Physical and Mental Requirements: It is needless to say that a foreman must have the physical and emotional capacity to carry his responsibilities and perform his duties with the vigor which the job requires.

Finding Prospects

Companies generally try to find people within their own organization who can be promoted to the position of foreman whenever a vacancy occurs. They do this because it has a definite bearing on the growth and development of foremen into better supervisors. When a man is promoted from the ranks to the position of foreman, he is given evidence that the company is trying to follow the policy of "promotion from within." This gives him the feeling that if he does a good job as foreman he may have a chance at some later date to be considered for an even better job. A foreman who feels he can look to his own company for advancement, rather than having to look to a competitor, is able for psychological reasons, to give more of himself to his job and his company. This procedure also helps stimulate job interest on the part of the foreman's employees because they too feel that if they do a good job where they are, they may later be advanced to the position of foreman. More and more employees are looking for jobs that offer career opportunities, and as long as a company holds to the policy of promotion from within, workers can feel that their present company offers career possibilities.

What Kind of Training?

Programs for training foremen take various forms. Among them are: programs designed to prepare candidates for promotion to the job of a foreman; programs designed to stimulate die development of existing foremen so they can do a better job; refresher courses for foremen who have already been trained; and programs designed to train foremen for higher positions in the organization.

The fact that foreman training is so strongly emphasized by industry does not mean that the foreman of today is lacking in capability. On the contrary, most foremen are capable, well-qualified people. However, attitudes of people are constantly changing, new labor relations philosophies are being developed, and new processes and new techniques are being introduced. It is only good business to expose foremen to training sessions which will give them the information necessary to keep abreast of the changing industrial picture. The primary reason why such careful attention has been given to the subject of foremen training in recent years is the long-unfilled need which resulted from the time when it was not felt necessary to train foremen at all. It was felt that this need could be adequately met through supervision of the foreman by his superiors. Here is another example of the fact that industrial philosophies and practices change.

A foreman on the job today already has a certain amount of leadership ability, organizational ability, understanding of people, technical skill, and mechanical ability. These are qualifications he has to possess if he is to hold down his job. He can't get production out on time without them. The question is: Can the foreman's ability to lead and understand people, and organize his shop, be improved with training designed to help him in these areas? The answer is: "Yes." Leaders from both large and small companies agree that training in foremanship can definitely help the foreman to develop his abilities and thereby enable him to do a better job in the plant. In addition, after a foreman has taken a course in leadership training, he needs refresher courses from time to time because under pressure of meeting schedules and deadlines even the most conscientious supervisor forgets or overlooks part of what he already knows. Experience proves that die art of getting things done through people is a subject which supervisors can, with profit, be coached in—at regular intervals.

The foreman also needs training in shop organization and in work simplification. There are certain basic principles of good organization which can be applied to most any department. Also, new techniques are developed from time to time which permit plant procedures to be simplified with a saving of time and money. Any foreman training program should deal with the subject of shop organization techniques because good organization reduces waste and production costs and improves employee morale.

Solving the Problem in Small Plants

Because of practical considerations, small plants are limited in their ability to develop and promote their own formal training programs for foremen. Nevertheless, many of them consider the need for this training to be of such importance that they are discovering ways and means for making it available in spite of limited resources. In general, small plants are working through one of four general methods.

1. Cooperation With Other Small Plants: In areas where a number of small plants are located, arrangement can often be made whereby several plants jointly hire a training specialist who develops a foreman training program designed to fit the particular needs of the cooperating plants. Such projects are financed by the cooperating firms on a joint basis. Arrangements of this type have proved successful in Chicago, Pittsburgh, and Philadelphia. The idea was developed with the help of management consulting firms.

2. Cooperation With Colleges and Universities: Some colleges and universities, in cooperation with small plants, have developed foreman and supervisory training programs designed to meet the needs of plants in their particular areas. These programs are usually offered in connection with adult training courses given by the colleges. Those who attend usually get the benefit of instruction both from college professors who have specialized in training problems and from industrial experts. While there are relatively few such arrangement—at least so far as foremen are concerned—plants that have participated in projects of this type regard them as most successful. An alternative method of training foreman is the home study course. Subjects taught by accredited home study schools include quality control, report writing, safety engineering, and others.

3. Use of Programs Developed By Larger Companies: Some small plants purchase foreman training programs from larger companies which are in the same general type of business. They use such programs to conduct training sessions under the

leadership of someone on their own staff. Some large companies are very generous in letting other companies use their material. While this arrangement has its disadvantages, it has been known to produce desirable results, especially where the directors of such training sessions are skilled in conference leadership techniques. Those who use this arrangement point out that, in the final analysis, foremen will train each other if (a) they have an adequate text upon which to base their discussions, and (b) the leader of the training sessions is gifted in stimulating group discussions in connection with problems which foreman as individuals face on their particular jobs.

Where a small company has a close relationship with one of the larger companies, arrangements can often be made whereby the small plant sends a member of its staff to attend the foreman training course of the large company. That person ultimately returns and serves as an instructor for foremen in his own plant. It should be noted, however, that training programs developed for large companies need to be modified if they are used in small plants.

4. Use of Supervisory Programs Developed By Management Associations: Some small plants solve their foreman training problem by making use of the staff facilities of national management associations. The assistance rendered by such organizations to small plants has produced excellent results. Among those associations which have taken an active interest in foremen training are the National Association of Manufacturers, some local Chambers of Commerce, the National Association of Foremen, the Foremen's League, and the American Management Association. These groups offer a variety of services which can and are being utilized by small companies as follows:

   a. Some have training specialists who are available to small businesses for the purpose of conducting foremen and supervisory training programs.
   b. Some have training specialists available as consultants of the purpose of helping small establishments set up their own training program.
   c. Some have foreman training programs of various types which small plants can use in conducting their own training sessions.
   d. Some offer a generalize type of foreman training through the use of foremen's clubs. Such clubs are designed to promote a better understanding by the foreman of his responsibilities as a member of management.

Measuring the Results

Since a training program for foremen deals with leadership and organizational problems, the results of the training can usually be measured only in terms of the foreman's performance on the job. There is no way to predict from classroom discussions how valuable the training will be to the company. The results of such training, if they are to be of value, must be reflected in the performance records of the foreman's department. If the course has been a success, proof will be found in increased ability to get work out in less time, with less expense, and with fewer employee grievances than previously. While it may take weeks for any results to become apparent, a good foreman training program will help to accomplish this objective. Following are the specific items by which the foreman's performance can be measured to determine what results have been obtained: overtime expense, number of production units which have been rejected, amount of material wasted, number of workers required to get the work out, number of hours the machines are utilized, the number and nature of employee grievances which are filed, and the amount of absenteeism. If the training program has been successful, there should in due time be an improvement in each of the categories listed above.

How Top Management Promotes Foreman Development

A training program alone is not sufficient to encourage the development of foremen to the maximum extent. After a foreman has completed his training, he wants to see evidence that his job is as important as the training program led him to believe. If he is to be regarded as a part of management, he wants to be given the authority, prestige, and recognition which goes with it. Once he has been given proper recognition, this tends to serve as a constant reminder of the importance of his job and encourages him to make greater efforts toward self-improvement on his own initiative.

There are several ways in which top management can provide the proper recognition to foremen:

1. Incentive Payments: Many firms have the policy of paying bonuses to their top management in proportion to their salaries, based upon how much profit the company makes each year. By spreading such bonus payments to all levels of management, foremen and other supervisors are made to feel that they really are a part of management and that the more efficiently they run their shops, the greater the chance that their annual bonuses will be increased.

2. Authority: It is not enough to spell out the duties and responsibilities of the foreman. He must be given suitable authority. Top management should also make it clear that they will back up the foreman in any decisions that he makes within the scope of his duties and responsibilities. This helps to promote the growth of the foreman because it keeps him alert to the fact that he is, in reality as well as title, a part of management.

3. Prestige: Top management can develop a sense of responsibility and job satisfaction in its foremen, by use of the following other devices:

    a. A bulletin from the president to all levels of management informing them of any major changes in company policy. It lets the foreman and other supervisors know that the top management prefers for supervisors to get the story direct rather than through the grapevine or the newspapers.

    b. Staff sessions called by top management of a small plant for the purpose of getting advice on company problems have proved effective in developing a broader sense of responsibility among foremen.

    c. Occasional banquet where all levels of management are invited for getting-acquainted purposes helps to stimulate job enthusiasm on the part of foremen.

A foreman who is properly trained and who enjoys proper recognition of his status is one of the most important people in industry today. The extent to which he develops his abilities to do the job expected of him is, in large measure, dependent upon how much interest top management in the small plant is willing to take in him.

www.ingramcontent.com/pod-product-compliance
Lightning Source LLC
Chambersburg PA
CBHW082211300426
44117CB00016B/2767